THE .

A SPIRITUAL PERSPECTIVE

BOOKS BY ALICE A. BAILEY

Initiation, Human and Solar
Letters on Occult Meditation
The Consciousness of the Atom
A Treatise on Cosmic Fire
The Light of the Soul
The Soul and its Mechanism
From Intellect to Intuition
A Treatise on White Magic
From Bethlehem to Calvary
Discipleship in the New Age–Vol. I
Discipleship in the New Age–Vol. II
Problems of Humanity
The Reappearance of the Christ
The Destiny of the Nations
Glamour: A World Problem
Telepathy and the Etheric Vehicle
The Unfinished Autobiography
Education in the New Age
The Externalisation of the Hierarchy

A Treatise on the Seven Rays:

Vol. I – Esoteric Psychology
Vol. II – Esoteric Psychology
Vol. III – Esoteric Astrology
Vol. IV – Esoteric Healing
Vol. V – The Rays and the Initiations

THE ANIMAL KINGDOM
A SPIRITUAL PERSPECTIVE

From the Writings of
Alice A. Bailey
and
The Tibetan Master, Djwhal Khul

LUCIS PUBLISHING COMPANY
New York

LUCIS PRESS LIMITED
London

This compilation is extracted from books by Alice A. Bailey for which the Lucis Trust holds copyrights.

First Printing 2005
Second Printing 2016

ISBN 978 085330 145 5
ISBN 0-85330-145-X

The fund which finances the publication of this book is controlled by the Lucis Trust, a tax-exempt, religious, educational corporation dedicated to the perpetuation of the teachings of the Tibetan and Alice A. Bailey.

The Lucis Publishing Companies are non-profit organisations owned by the Lucis Trust. No royalties are paid on this book.

LUCIS PUBLISHING COMPANY
120 Wall Street, New York, NY 10005

LUCIS PRESS LIMITED.
Suite 54, 3 Whitehall Court, London SW1A 2EF

www.lucistrust.org

PRINTED IN THE UNITED STATES OF AMERICA

EXTRACT FROM A STATEMENT
BY THE TIBETAN

Published August 1934

Suffice it to say, that I am a Tibetan disciple of a certain degree, and this tells you but little, for all are disciples from the humblest aspirant up to, and beyond, the Christ Himself. I live in a physical body like other men, on the borders of Tibet, and at times (from the exoteric standpoint) preside over a large group of Tibetan lamas, when my other duties permit. It is this fact that has caused it to be reported that I am an abbot of this particular lamasery. Those associated with me in the work of the Hierarchy (and all true disciples are associated in this work) know me by still another name and office. A.A.B. knows who I am and recognises me by two of my names.

I am a brother of yours, who has travelled a little longer upon the Path than has the average student, and has therefore incurred greater responsibilities. I am one who has wrestled and fought his way into a greater measure of light than has the aspirant who will read this article, and I must therefore act as a transmitter of the light, no matter what the cost. I am not an old man, as age counts among the teachers, yet I am not young or inexperienced. My work is to teach and spread the knowledge of the Ageless Wisdom wherever I can find a response, and I have been doing this for many years. I seek also to help the Master M. and the Master K.H. whenever opportunity offers, for I have been long connected with Them and with Their work. In all the above, I have told you much; yet at the same time I have told you nothing which would lead you to offer me that blind obedience and the foolish devotion which the emotional aspirant offers to the Guru and Master Whom he is as yet unable to contact. Nor will he make that desired contact until he has transmuted emotional devotion into unselfish service to humanity – not to the Master.

The books that I have written are sent out with no claim for their acceptance. They may, or may not, be correct, true and useful. It is for you to ascertain their truth by right practice and by the exercise of the intuition. Neither I nor A.A.B. is the least interested in having them acclaimed as inspired writings, or in having anyone speak of them (with bated breath) as being the work of one of the Masters. If they present truth in such a way that it follows sequentially upon that already offered in the world teachings, if the information given raises the aspiration and the will-to-serve from the plane of the emotions to that of the mind (the plane whereon the Masters *can* be found) then they will have served their purpose. If the teaching conveyed calls forth a response from the illumined mind of the worker in the world, and brings a flashing forth of his intuition, then let that teaching be accepted. But not otherwise. If the statements meet with eventual corroboration, or are deemed true under the test of the Law of Correspondences, then that is well and good. But should this not be so, let not the student accept what is said.

THE GREAT INVOCATION

From the point of Light within the Mind of God
Let light stream forth into the minds of men.
Let Light descend on Earth.

From the point of Love within the Heart of God
Let love stream forth into the hearts of men.
May Christ return to Earth.

From the centre where the Will of God is known
Let purpose guide the little wills of men –
The purpose which the Masters know and serve.

From the centre which we call the race of men
Let the Plan of Love and Light work out.
And may it seal the door where evil dwells.

Let Light and Love and Power restore the Plan on Earth.

"The above Invocation or Prayer does not belong to any person or group but to all Humanity. The beauty and the strength of this Invocation lies in its simplicity, and in its expression of certain central truths which all men, innately and normally, accept – the truth of the existence of a basic Intelligence to Whom we vaguely give the name of God; the truth that behind all outer seeming, the motivating power of the universe is Love; the truth that a great Individuality came to earth, called by Christians, the Christ, and embodied that love so that we could understand; the truth that both love and intelligence are effects of what is called the Will of God; and finally the self-evident truth that only through *humanity* itself can the Divine Plan work out."

ALICE A. BAILEY

TABLE OF CONTENTS

Page

KEYNOTE:

... God loves – without distinction and irrespective of race or creed. To that Great Life naught matters but humanity and its perfecting, because upon humanity depends the salvation of all the kingdoms in nature.

The Externalisation of the Hierarchy, p. 477

The two problems which are of immediate concern to mankind in relation to the animal kingdom are:

The problem of human relations and responsibility.
The problem of animal individualisation.

Esoteric Psychology I, p. 254

HUMAN RELATIONS
AND RESPONSIBILITIES

Just as God is the Macrocosm for all the kingdoms in Nature, so man is the Macrocosm for all the sub-human kingdoms.

A Treatise on Cosmic Fire, p. 7

A grub or worm working out its little life in a mass of decaying substance is as much a spiritual manifestation as an initiate working out his destiny in a mass of rapidly changing human forms. It is all manifested Deity; it is all divine expression and all a form of sensitive awareness and of response to environment, and therefore a form of conscious expression.

Esoteric Psychology I, p. 17

Broadly speaking, the work of the human kingdom is to transmit energy to the lower kingdoms in Nature, whilst the work of the Hierarchy, in its relation to the human kingdom, is to transmit energies from the spiritual realm, from other planetary centres, and from the solar system.

A Treatise on White Magic, p. 291

The Kingdom of God is . . . simply and solely what it claims to be: a vast and integrated group of soul-infused persons, radiating love and spiritual intention, motivated by goodwill, and rooted in the human kingdom, as the kingdom of men is rooted in and is a break-away from the animal kingdom.

Discipleship in the New Age II, pp. 407-08

The spiritual energy and not just the consciousness or sentient energy pours through Man, the instrument of divine Life, and the custodian of forces, to be held and used for the other and lower kingdoms in nature.

A Treatise on White Magic, p. 285

With that great hierarchical unit which we call the animal kingdom, the third kingdom in nature, man is definitely related through the medium of his animal, etheric and astral bodies.

Education in the New Age, p. 126

The emotional body is at this time the most important body in the Personality for several reasons. It is a complete unit, unlike the physical and mental bodies; it is the centre of polarisation for the majority of the human family; it is the most difficult body to control, and is practically the very last body to be completely subjugated. The reason for this is that the vibration of desire has dominated, not only the human kingdom but also the animal and vegetable kingdoms in a lesser sense, so that the evolving inner man has to work against inclinations set up in three kingdoms.

Letters on Occult Meditation, p. 98

Men should remember that through the power of their thoughts and their spoken words they definitely produce effects upon other human beings functioning on the three planes of human evolution and upon the entire animal kingdom. The separative and maleficent thoughts of man are largely responsible for the savage nature of wild beasts, and the destructive quality of some of nature's processes, including certain phenomena, such as plague and famine.

A Treatise on Cosmic Fire, p. 889

Tuberculosis, which was devastatingly rampant at a certain stage in Atlantean times, is nevertheless a disease which has been *generated* principally in our Aryan race, and one which we are bequeathing to the animal kingdom and are sharing with them. This is beginning to be realised. So close, however, is the relation between men and animals (particularly the domestic animals) that they today share with men practically all his ailments in some form or another, sometimes recognisable and sometimes not.

Esoteric Healing, p. 59

In the animal kingdom the first dim indication of sorrow and pain is seen, whilst in the higher and the domesticated animals these two educating processes are still more clearly indicated. Man's work with the animals is potent in results, and will lead eventually to a re-opening of the door into the human kingdom. Some of the work already done by man has outstripped divine expectation and may warrant a hastening of the Plan.

Esoteric Psychology I, p. 251

The third type of activity which should occupy the attention of humanity, and one as yet little understood, is that it should act as a transmitting centre of spiritual forces – soul force and spiritual energy united and combined – to the prisoners of the planet and to the lives, held in embodied existence in the other kingdoms of nature. Human beings are apt to be primarily concerned with their higher group relations, with their return to the Father's home, and with the trend which we call "upwards" and away from the phenomenal world. They are principally occupied with the finding of the centre within the form aspect, that which we call the soul, and, having found it, with the work then of acquainting themselves with that soul and thus finding peace. This is right and in line with divine intention but it is not all of the plan for man, and when this remains the prime objective, a man is dangerously near falling into the snare of spiritual selfishness and separateness.

When the centre is found by any human being and he becomes at-one with, and enters into relation with his soul, then he automatically shifts his position in the human family and – again speaking in symbols – finds himself part of the centre of light and understanding which we call, esoterically, the occult hierarchy, the cloud of witnesses, the disciples of the Christ, and other names according to the trend of the disciple's convictions. This hierarchy is also attempting to externalise itself in the form of the group of World Workers, and when a man has found his soul and the principle of unity is sufficiently revealed to him he shifts also into this more exoteric group. All who find the centre do not as yet link up with both the interior and exterior groups. Then he is pledged to the magical work, to the salvaging of souls, to the releasing of the prisoners of the planet. This is the goal for humanity as a whole, and when all the sons of men have attained the objective, these prisoners will be released. The reason for this will be that the magical work will be carried forward intelligently and perfectly and human beings in group formation will act as transmitters of pure spiritual energy, which will vivify every form in every kingdom in nature.

A Treatise on White Magic, pp. 529-30

The fourth Creative Hierarchy, the human Kingdom, is the agent through which eventually the energies of Shamballa and of the Hierarchy will be focussed for the redeeming of the life of all the sub-human kingdoms. This can only take place when humanity can work with the focussed will, engendered by the life of Shamballa, inspired by love, fostered by the Hierarchy and expressed through the intellect which humanity itself has developed – all of these used dynamically and consciously under the pressure of that which is higher and greater than Shamballa itself.

Esoteric Astrology, p. 617

We are considering the expression of the Shamballa force in terms of Will, i.e., of divine purpose, latent in the mind of God since the beginning of time and the dawn of creation. In God's mind, that idea is seen whole and complete.

In manifestation it is a gradual, self-revealing evolutionary and demonstrated activity. We know somewhat of the intelligence aspect of God. It is revealed in the living activity of substance. Of the love of that Great Thinker, we are learning slowly and its revelation has reached the stage where the human mind can contrast its mode of living activity with the visioned and sensed love of Deity, expressed as yet by the desire for right human relations and right treatment of all that is non-human.

Esoteric Astrology, pp. 591-92

The purpose, consequently, for the very existence of the fourth kingdom in nature (as a transmitting agent for the higher spiritual energies to the three lower kingdoms) will begin to appear, and men, in group formation, will consciously begin this work of "saving" – in the esoteric sense, needless to say – these other grouped lives. The Macrocosm with its purpose and incentives will for the first time begin to reflect itself into the human kingdom in a new and more potent manner, and this in its turn will become the macrocosm of the three lesser states of conscious lives – the animal, the vegetable and the mineral kingdoms.

Esoteric Healing, pp. 586-87

Harmful magnetic conditions, as the result of man's wrong handling of force are the causes of evil in the world around us, including the three sub-human kingdoms. How can we, as individuals, change this? By the development in ourselves of Harmlessness. . . .

Breadth of vision, inclusiveness of understanding and a widened horizon are the preliminary essentials to all work under the guidance of the hierarchy of adepts; the stabilizing of the consciousness in the one life, and the recognition of the basic unity of all creation has to be somewhat developed before any one can be trusted with certain knowledges and Words of Power and the manipulation of those forces which bring the subjective reality into outer manifestation.

A Treatise on White Magic, pp. 101-02

He grasps, gropingly at first, the idea of the unity of the Life, and its manifestation as the Brotherhood existing between all forms of that divine Life. This subjective ideal gradually leads to an appreciation of the way in which this essential relationship can work out practically. This can be seen finding its expression in the great humanitarian efforts, in the organisations for the relief of human and animal suffering, and in world wide efforts for the betterment of the internal relations of nations, religions and groups.

Ibid, pp. 93-4

The knowing of the fifth kingdom in nature through the medium of the consciousness of the fourth and the sacrifice of the fourth kingdom to the fifth, of the human being to the soul and of humanity to the kingdom of God, is the parallel (on a higher turn of the spiral) of the sacrifice of the third kingdom, the animal kingdom, to the fourth, the human kingdom. Thus it proceeds down the scale – sacrifice always of the lower to the higher.

The Rays and the Initiations, p. 129

There is a constant shifting in the state of the planetary consciousness and this, though implemented from Shamballa, is produced by humanity itself; this unfolding human consciousness leads mankind eventually out of the fourth kingdom in nature into the fifth, the hierarchy of souls, and – at the same time – raises the level of consciousness in all the three subhuman kingdoms. This series of happenings will remain for a long time inexplicable to man, though the results can be seen in the effect which humanity has had on the animal kingdom, through domestication; on the vegetable kingdom, through specialisation and science; and on the mineral kingdom, through the skilled utilisation of metals and the widespread use of the mineral products of the earth.

The Rays and the Initiations, pp. 369-70

Men are so apt to regard their own lives and destiny and the unfoldment of the human consciousness as the factor of only and paramount importance upon Earth and in the evolutionary processes of the planet. These conditions are of importance, but they are not the only factors of importance, nor does humanity stand alone and isolated. Humanity occupies a midway point between the subhuman and the superhuman kingdoms, and each of these groups of evolving lives has its own important destiny – important to all contained within the group ring-pass-not. They have their own chosen and differing modes, methods and ways of achievement. Just as individual man has to learn the art or science of relationship to other men and to his environment, so humanity as a whole has to learn its relationship to that which lies above and beyond mankind and with that which is below and left behind. This involves a sense of proportion which can be attained only by the mind principle in man and by those who are beginning to be mentally polarised. This sense of proportion will reveal to men their place upon the ladder of evolution and lead them to the recognition of the peculiar destiny and unique goals of other kingdoms in nature, including the fifth kingdom, the Kingdom of God, the spiritual Hierarchy of our planet.

Ibid., pp. 333-34

[I]t should be possible, from the standpoint of each kingdom of nature, to aid the transmuting process of all lesser atoms. This is so, even though it is not recognised; it is only when the human kingdom is reached that it is possible for an entity consciously and intelligently to do two things:

First: aid in the transmutation of his own positive atomic centre from the human into the spiritual.

Second: assist at the transmutation

a. From the lower mineral forms into the higher forms.
b. From the mineral forms into the vegetable.
c. From vegetable forms into the animal forms.
d. From animal forms into the human or consciously and definitely to bring about individualisation.

That it is not done as yet is due to the danger of imparting the necessary knowledge. The adepts understand the transmuting process in the three worlds, and in the four kingdoms of nature, which make them a temporary esoteric three and exoteric four.

Man will eventually work with the three kingdoms but, only when brotherhood is a practice and not a concept.

A Treatise on Cosmic Fire, pp. 479-80

The soil of the planet itself is a major cause of disease and of contamination. For untold aeons, the bodies of men and of animals have been laid away in the ground; that soil is consequently impregnated with the germs and the results of disease and this in a far subtler form than is surmised. The germs of ancient known and unknown diseases are to be found in the layers of the soil and the subsoil; these can still produce virulent trouble if presented with proper conditions. Let me state that Nature never intended that bodies would be buried in the ground. The animals die and their bodies return to the dust, but return purified by the rays of the sun and by the breezes which blow and disperse. The sun can cause death as well as life, and the most virulent germs and bacteria cannot retain their potency if submitted to the dry heat of the sun's rays. Moisture and darkness foster disease as it emanates from and is nourished by bodies from whence the life aspect has been drawn. When, in all countries throughout the world, the rule is to submit dead forms to the "ordeal by fire," and when this has become a universal and persistent habit, we shall then see a great diminution of disease and a much healthier world.

Esoteric Healing, pp. 250-51

[T]here are forces present in nature which are in the nature of left-overs, [which give] the clue to much of the puzzling side of manifestation, to the cruelty and death, the suffering, and the agony which are seen in the vegetable and animal kingdoms. In the term animal kingdom I include man's physical body.

A Treatise on Cosmic Fire, p. 1096

The animal kingdom has a peculiar relation to the fourth kingdom in nature, and the unfolding of the animal consciousness proceeds along lines paralleling, yet dissimilar to that of the human being who is beginning to respond to the kingdom of souls, the fifth kingdom. It is the karma and destiny of the fourth kingdom to be the impressing agent for the third; the problem is complicated, however, by the fact that the animal kingdom antedates the human and had, therefore, generated a measure of karma – both good and evil – prior to the appearance of mankind. The "impressing process" carried forward by humanity is modified and often negated by two factors:

1. Human ignorance and selfishness, plus inability to work consciously and intelligently with the embryonic minds within animal forms; this is true except in a few (a very few) cases which involve the domestic animals. When humanity is itself further

advanced, its intelligent impression upon the consciousness of the animal kingdom will produce planetary results. At present this is not so. It will only come when the animal kingdom (as a result of human understanding) becomes invocative.

2. The self-generated karma of the animal kingdom which is largely being worked off in its relation to mankind today. The karmic entity – holding a type of rule within the third kingdom – is a part of the planetary Dweller on the Threshold.

Telepathy and the Etheric Vehicle, p. 79

The ameliorative and palliative and curative work of medicine and surgery are proved beyond all controversial discussion. The methods employed, such as the vivisection of animals, may rightly cause distress. In spite of all this the indebtedness of mankind to the medical profession is great, and the service rendered to humanity by the profession does largely offset the evil.

Esoteric Healing, p. 28

2nd Aspect . . . Love, the dominating force of the soul life; through this possession and this type of energy, the soul can be en rapport with all souls. Through the emotional body, the soul can be in touch with all animal or subhuman souls, through its work on its own plane, with the meditating souls of all men. . . .

A Treatise on White Magic, p. 40

The soul is the perceiving entity produced through the union of Father-Spirit and Mother-Matter. It is that which in the vegetable world, for instance, produces response to the sun's rays, and the unfolding of the bud; it is that in the animal kingdom which enables it to love its master, hunt its prey, and follow out its instinctual life; it is that in man which makes him aware of his environment and his group, which enables him to live his life in the three worlds of his normal evolution as the onlooker, the perceiver, the actor. This it is which enables him eventually to discover that this soul in him is dual and that part of him responds to the animal soul and part of him recognises his divine soul. The majority however, at this time will be found to be functioning fully as neither purely animal nor purely divine, but can be regarded as human souls.

Ibid., p. 36-37

Men will finally be taught their responsibility to the animal kingdom. This will be brought about in three ways:

1. Man's truer understanding of his own animal nature.
2. A comprehension of the laws of individualisation, and the effect of the influence of the fourth, or human, kingdom upon the third, or animal, kingdom.
3. The work of an Avatar of a lesser order Who will come in the beginning of the next century to reveal to man his relationship to the third kingdom. His way is being prepared by the many who in these days are developing public interest through the various societies for the benefit and protection of animals, and through the many stories to be found in books and current periodicals.

A Treatise on Cosmic Fire, pp. 813-14

INSTINCT – INTELLECT – INTUITION

relates *unites* *reveals*
animal *human* *divine*
body *mind* *spirit*

Instinct relates man to the animal world, intellect unites him to his fellow men, whilst the intuition reveals to him the life of divinity.

A Treatise on White Magic, p. 411

In the earlier period [an earlier solar system] the effects in manifestation of the divine Flame were so remote and deeply hidden as to be scarcely recognisable, though dimly there. Its correspondence can be seen in the animal kingdom, in which instinct holds the intuition in latency, and the Spirit dimly overshadows. Yet all is part of a divine whole.

A Treatise on Cosmic Fire, pp. 57-58

In the animal these five senses exist but, as the thinking correlating faculty is lacking, as the "relation between" the self and the not-self is but little developed, we will not concern ourselves with them at this juncture. The senses in the animal kingdom are *group faculty* and demonstrate as racial instinct.

Ibid., p. 186

In the bulk of humanity the sacral centre and the solar plexus govern the life, and that is why desire for material living and for the sex life are so closely blended. The solar plexus in the animal is the brain and governs all the instinctual reactions, but is not so closely allied with the purely sex expression as it is in the human being.

A Treatise on White Magic, p. 310

[T]he instinctual nature, as it develops in the three kingdoms (animal, human and divine) is, in fact, that which develops stage by stage into what we call consciousness; it is in reality, the development of a gradual expansion of capacity to be aware of the environment, whatever that environment may be. The herd instinct of the animal is, for instance, the embryonic unfoldment of what is later recognised by the intellect as group consciousness. These higher developments are brought about by the application of the intellect and a change in the motivating power. The same idea can be traced in connection with all the instincts.

Esoteric Psychology II, p. 563

A mechanism in the natural body comes into use in two ways: First, its use is involuntary, and there is no comprehension of how, or why, or when, the apparatus is used. An animal employs a mechanism, analogous in many respects to that employed by man. He sees, and hears and functions organically along similar lines to the human, but lacks the mental understanding and the linking of cause and effect which are characteristic of the higher kingdom in nature.

A Treatise on White Magic, p. 165

Objective or exoteric information is largely that obtained or ascertained by men in the Hall of Learning by means of the five senses, and by experiment. Experiment in due course of time and after many cycles of incarnation is transmuted into experience, and this produces eventually that which we call instinct, or the habitual reaction of some type of consciousness to a given set of circumstances, or of environment. These two factors of the senses and of experimental contact can be seen working out in the animal and human kingdoms; the difference between the two exists in the ability of the man consciously to remember, apprehend, anticipate, and utilise the fruits of past experience, and thus influence the present and prepare for the future. He employs the physical brain for this purpose. An animal likewise has an instinctual memory, apprehension, and an embryo anticipation, but (lacking mind) he is unable to adjust them to circumstances in the sense of prearrangement, and lacks the capacity consciously to utilise, and thus reap, the benefit of past events, and to learn from experience in the manner which a man does. The animal uses the solar plexus in the same way that a man uses the brain; it is the organ of instinct. . . .

As time progresses and man reaches a fair state of evolution, mind is more rapidly developed, and a new factor comes gradually into play. Little by little the intuition, or the transcendental mind, begins to function, and eventually supersedes the lower or concrete mind. It then utilises the physical brain as a receiving plate, but at the same time develops certain centres in the head, and thus transfers the zone of its activity from the physical brain to the higher head centres, existing in etheric matter. For the mass of humanity, this will be effected during the opening up of the etheric subplanes during the next two races. This is paralleled in the animal kingdom by the gradual transference of the zone of activity from the solar plexus to the rudimentary brain, and its gradual development by the aid of manas.

A Treatise on Cosmic Fire, pp. 286-87

As is well known, the five kingdoms of nature on the evolutionary arc might be defined as follows: – the mineral kingdom, the vegetable kingdom, the animal kingdom, the human kingdom, and the spiritual kingdom. All these kingdoms embody some type of consciousness, and it is the work of the Hierarchy to develop these types to perfection through the adjustment of karma, through the agency of force, and through the providing of right conditions. Some idea of the work may be gained if we briefly summarize the different aspects of consciousness to be developed in the various kingdoms. ...

In the *animal kingdom* this rudimentary activity and feeling are increased, and symptoms (if it might be so inadequately expressed) are to be found of the first aspect, or embryonic will and purpose; we may call it hereditary instinct, but it works out in fact as purpose in nature.

It has been wisely stated by H. P. Blavatsky that man is the macrocosm for the three lower kingdoms, for in him these three lines of development are synthesised and come to their full fruition. He is verily and indeed intelligence, actively and wonderfully manifested; He is incipient love and wisdom, even though as yet they may be but the goal of his endeavour; and he has that embryonic, dynamic, initiating will which will come to a fuller development after he has entered into the fifth kingdom.

Initiation, Human and Solar, pp. 21-2

It is only possible to suggest to the intelligent student that the light of his soul (reflected in his mind) and the energy of form (as expressed in his etheric body) are for him, in the realm of temporary duality, his two basic realities. . . . Any true aspirant knows that his spiritual progress can be gauged in terms of his freedom from this illusion and of his release into the clear air and pure light of his spiritual consciousness. In its consciousness, the animal kingdom works with the second of these two basic realities, and for it the life of the etheric body and the force which governs the animal or material nature are the prime expression of truth. Yet the animal is beginning to sense dimly the world of illusion and possesses certain psychic powers and senses which recognise yet fail to interpret the astral plane. The veil of illusion is beginning to fall before the eyes of the animal but it knows it not. . . .

As far as humanity is concerned, it is the time wherein man is enveloped in mist and fog, and lost in the miasmas arising out of the ground (symbol of the foundational nature of the animal kingdom). Yet at times this stage is seen to be unreal as the dawning light of the spiritual consciousness pierces through the surrounding darkness. It is the interlude between the dominance of the animal consciousness and that of the spiritual, and this interlude of astral illusion is only known in the human family. There is no astral plane except in the consciousness of the fourth kingdom in nature, for man is "under illusion" in a sense different to the conscious awareness of any other kingdom – subhuman or superhuman.

A Treatise on White Magic, pp. 612-14

The sentient souls of animals and of men are subconsciously aware of factors such as:

1. The vastness and therefore the sensed oppression of the Whole.
2. The pressure of all other lives and existences.
3. The working of inexorable Law.
4. The sense of imprisonment, of limitation, and of consequent inadequacy.

In these factors, growing out of the manifested process itself and persisting and growing in potency during the ages, are found the causes of all modern fear and the basis of all terror, above all that which is purely psychological and not just the instinctual fear of the animal.

Ibid., pp. 298-99

[E]ach kingdom in nature acts in two ways:

1. As the liberator of the kingdom of forms which has not reached its particular stage of conscious awareness.
2. As the prison house of lives that have transitted into it from the level of consciousness next beneath it.

Let it be remembered always that each field of awareness in its boundaries constitutes a prison, and that the objective of all work of liberation is to release the consciousness and expand its field of contacts. Where there are boundaries of any kind, where a field of influence is circumscribed, and where the radius of contact is limited there you have a prison. Ponder on this statement for it holds much of truth. Where there is an apprehension of a vision and of a wide unconquered territory of contacts then there will inevitably be a sense of imprisonment and of cramping. Where there is realisation of worlds to conquer, of truths to be learnt, of conquests to be made, of desires to be achieved, of knowledges to be mastered, there you will have a festering sense of limitation, goading on the aspirant to renewed effort and driving the living entity on along the path of evolution. Instinct, governing the vegetable and animal kingdoms, develops into intellect in the human family. Later intellect merges into intuition and intuition into illumination. When the superhuman consciousness is evoked these two – intuition and illumination – take the place of instinct and of intelligence.

Ibid., pp. 534-35

The task of humanity falls primarily into three divisions of labour. Three groups of prisoners can be released and will eventually find their way out of their prison house through the instrumentality of man. Already human beings are working in all three fields.

1. Prisoners within the human form. This involves working with one's fellow men.
2. Prisoners within the animal kingdom, and already much is being done in this field.
3. Prisoners within the forms of the vegetable world. A beginning has been made here.

A Treatise on White Magic., pp. 535-36

In touching upon the work of humanity in releasing the units of which it is constructed, and in releasing the prisoners in the vegetable and animal kingdoms, I want to point out two things, both of profound importance:

First, in order to release the "prisoners of the planet" that come under the title of *subhuman*, man has to work under the influence of the *intuition*; when working to release his fellow men he has to know the meaning of *Illumination.*

[Second] . . . I have given no specific rules for releasing the prisoners of the planet. . . .

Ibid., p. 537

Light

Every human being who reaches the goal of light and wisdom automatically has a field of influence which extends both up and down, and which reaches both inwards to the source of light and outwards into the "fields of darkness". When he has thus attained he will become a conscious centre of life giving force, and will be so without effort. He will stimulate, energise and vivify to fresh efforts all lives that he contacts, be they his fellow aspirants, or an animal, or a flower. He will act as a transmitter of light in the darkness. He will dispel the glamour around him and let in the radiance of reality.

When large numbers of the sons of men can so act, then the human family will enter upon its destined work of planetary service. Its mission is to act as a bridge between the world of spirit and the world of material forms. All grades of matter meet in man, and all the states of consciousness are possible to him. Mankind can work in all directions and lift the subhuman kingdoms into heaven and bring heaven down to earth.

Heaven to earth

Ibid., p. 538

When men are universally en rapport with the custodians of the plan and their minds and brains are illumined by the light of the intuition, of the soul and of the universal mind, when they can train themselves to respond intelligently to the timely impulses which cyclically emanate from the inner side of life, then there will be a steady adjustment between life and form and a rapid amelioration of world conditions. It is an interesting point to bear in mind that the first effect of the response of the more advanced of the sons of men to the formulas as translated and transmitted by the Knowers will be the establishing of right relations between the four kingdoms in nature, and right relations between units and groups in the human family. A step in this direction is being made. Relations between the four spheres of activity which we call human, animal, vegetable and mineral are now badly adjusted because the energy of matter is primarily the governing factor. In the human kingdom, the working of this energy demonstrates in what we call selfishness. In the animal kingdom, it demonstrates in what we call cruelty, though, where the sense of responsibility is nonexistent and only instinctual and temporary parental responsibility is found, there is no criticism to be given. In the vegetable kingdom this maladjustment expresses itself during this planetary period of misuse as disease.

A Treatise on White Magic, p. 462

The spheres of activity

harmlessness
helpfulness
selflessness
fearlessness

ignorance
learning
belief
knowing

INDIVIDUALISATION

When the animal kingdom, viewing it from the angle of the whole and not from the angle of species, had reached a particular stage of development, then there was an inrush into the planetary life of the energy of all the seven rays simultaneously. This occurs very rarely and the tremendous stimulation then undergone by the sensitive forms of life (and of these the animal was at that time the most sensitive), produced the emergence of a new form, that of infant humanity. It was the reaction of that kingdom, as expressed through its indwelling life, the animal Being (who is the informing Life of that kingdom in nature), which produced individualisation in the more advanced animal-man of the time.

What really occurred was a reaction throughout the entire animal kingdom to the inpouring of the three major types of energy, which expressed themselves through the usual seven types and thus called forth response from those forms of life which were energised through the medium of the three major centres – heart, head and throat – of the

25

Being who is the informing life. A tremendous surging up-
ward and a going-forth in response ensued, which enabled
a new kingdom to emerge.

Esoteric Psychology II , pp. 212-13

The relation of the animals to man has been purely physical
in the long past ages. Animals preyed upon men in the days
when animal-man was but little removed from them. It is
oft forgotten that there was a stage in human development
when animal-man and the existent forms of animal life
lived in a much closer relation than today. Then, only the
fact of individualisation separated them. It was, however,
an individualisation so little realised that the difference between the mindless animal (so-called) and infant humanity
was scarcely appreciable. In those distant aeons, much transpired which has been lost in the dark silence of the past.
The animal world was then far more potent than the human,
men were helpless before the onslaughts of the animals,
and the devastation wrought by animals upon early animal-
men in mid-Lemurian days was terrible and appalling. Little nomadic groups of human beings would be completely
wiped out, age after age, by the powerful animal life of the
period, and though instinct taught the animal-men to take
certain precautions, it was an instinct but little removed
from that found in their enemies. It was only as the millenia
of years passed away, and human intelligence and cunning
began to assert themselves, that humanity became more
powerful than the animals and in its turn devastated the animal kingdom. Up until two hundred years ago the toll of

life exacted by the animal world from the human, in the forests of the western continents, in Africa, in the primeval lands of Australia and in the islands of the tropic seas, was incalculable. This is a fact often forgotten in the sentimentality of a moment, but it lies at the root of man's cruelty to animals. It is but the inevitable karma of the animal kingdom working out. The question must be viewed from a larger scale than has hitherto been the case, and its true historic values must be better understood before man can intelligently decide what constitutes his problem of responsibility and how it should be met and solved.

Esoteric Psychology I, pp. 256 -57

From one interesting angle the battle of the opposites upon the lower spiral, in which the physical body in its two aspects is concerned, can be seen taking place in the animal kingdom. In this process, human beings act as the agents of discipline, and the domesticated animals, which are forced to conform to human control, are wrestling (even if unconsciously from our point of view) with the problem of this lower pair of opposites. Their battle is fought out through the medium of the dense physical body and the etheric forces, and in this way a higher aspiration is brought into expression. This produces in them the experience which we call "individualisation," wherein the seed of personality is sown. On the human battlefield, the kurukshetra, the higher aspect of the soul begins to dominate, producing the process of divine-human integration which we call "initiation." Ponder on this.

Glamour: A World Problem, pp. 87-8

It is of course apparent that the effect of the interrelation existing between animals and men is to produce in the former that step forward which is called individualisation. This event is a consummation of the process of transfusion, and indicates the appearance of the three divine aspects in a unit of life in form. A son of God, a Lord of dedicated and directed Will, is born, and the third divine principle of purposive energy is fused with the other two and brings about an entire reorganisation within the animal form. As esotericists have long pointed out, individualisation is a great planetary experiment, and when it was instituted it superseded the earlier method, employed upon the Moon, wherein the urge to reach out and on (called aspiration where man is concerned) was the method employed. This really means that, when the evolving life within the form had reached a certain stage of growth in sentiency and awareness, and the inner urge was adequately strong, the life forced itself into contact with another stream of divine expression, with another major ray manifestation. This union of various activities caused a new being to emerge into manifestation. This is the basic truth lying behind the ideas put out at this time and classified under the general term "emergent evolution." It governs still in many departments of nature, and used to govern the appearance of human beings upon the planet. The urge and the development are from within the organism itself, and are the result of growth, of a reaching out and of an expansion.

But the method usually employed at this time is in the nature of a great second ray experiment. This involves an activity from without, from above, from a higher or from the divine side, if such a use of relatively meaningless words can avail to depict the process. The urge or push in this case does not originate from the lower two expressions or earlier fusions of divine energies. It is the higher aspect of divinity which takes the initiative and which, through a stimulation applied from without, causes a response from the life in form. Hence the process is really in the nature of an initiation.

The animals which individualise are, in every case today, the domestic animals, such as the horse, the dog, the elephant and the cat. These four groups of animals are at this time in the "process of transfusion", as it is occultly called, and one by one the life units are prepared and brought to the door of that peculiar initiatory process which we call – for lack of a better term – individualisation. They wait in that condition until the word goes forth that that door may be passed which will admit them to

> ". . . the triple way that leads to the dual road, by treading which they stand at last before the golden door. This final door ushers them upon that Path which is the one, alone and single, and disappears into the Light".

> *Old Commentary*

The factors which determine individualisation are several in number, and some of them might be enumerated as follows:

1. The response of the instinctive nature of the animal to the mental atmosphere of the human being, or beings, with which it is surrounded.

within
without
beyond

2. The outgoing love and interest of the people to which the animal is attached by the bonds of affection or of service.
3. The ray impulses which are active at any time. These are, amongst others:
    a. The ray of the animal itself. Elephants are upon the first ray; dogs are expressions of the second ray; the cat is a third ray life manifestation, and the horse is sixth ray. Animals upon other rays are not yet ready for individualisation.*
    b. The ray of the particular person or persons with whom the animal is associated.
    c. The ray or rays of a particular periodic cycle.

I could give you the techniques with which the guardians of the races and kingdoms work when seeking to bring about individualisation, but of what purpose would it be and what use would such information serve? Each ray affects the units found upon it at such a crisis as individualisation in a manner differing from any other ray; each ray finds its point of prime contact through one or other of the centres in the etheric bodies of animals and men. It must be remembered in this connection that, in the animal, four centres are functioning, and three are present but latent in their effect and use. The process followed is

---

* See page 44 for a different enumeration of the rays. The apparent contradiction may be due to the use of the word "ray" without indicating whether a major ray, one of the seven subrays of a major ray, or a complementary ray is implied. – *The Publishers*

that each ray works or pours its energy through one or other of the centres in the etheric body of that Entity Who informs an entire kingdom in nature, and then through that particular centre galvanises the individualising unit into the needed activity. Later, when the ray effects, psychologically speaking, are better understood, and the centres, with their seven ray vibrations, have been more deeply studied, it will be found that through a particular centre and along a particular ray vibration, forms of life and centres of consciousness can be contacted and known. This applies to all forms in all kingdoms, subhuman or superhuman. One of the first ways in which man is learning this truth is through the discovery of that vibration – emanating from a particular Master – which produces a reaction in himself, and which calls forth a response. Thus he is enabled to find out upon which ray his soul is found and to which ray group he should be attracted. This is of importance to the aspirant, and should be considered more carefully than has hitherto been the case, for by it the aspirant determines the nature and the quality of his soul type, and of the centre through which he (occultly speaking) goes out upon the Path. He discovers likewise the group of forms and of lives with which he is linked, to which he must render service, and by which he can be served.

The relation of man to the animals is, as we have seen, physical, emotional and increasingly mental. Each race of men, in its turn, and working under the ray influences, produces definite effects upon the three subhuman kingdoms. Through humanity, when the great experiment of

(margin note: Souls)

individualisation was initiated, the energies or ray influences from the superhuman kingdoms were focussed and the great function of humanity began, which is the transmitting of the ray forces cyclically.

Esoteric Psychology I, pp. 258-62

(margin note: Trans Migration of Souls)

In relation to the animal kingdom it might be said that the key whereby entrance is effected into the human kingdom is that of *instinct*. This instinct, towards the final stages of the animal's evolution, and as it becomes more and more detached from the group soul[1], becomes transmuted into mentality, or into that embryo mind which is latent in animal-man, and which simply needed the stimulating vibration which emanated from the Earth's Primary to be fanned into something definitely human. We must always bear in mind that the method of individualisation on this globe was not the one followed on others, and that many of the present advanced units of humanity individualised normally, and through the driving force of evolution itself. They found (to express it as far as possible in terms of fire), their opposite electrical pole through the activity of animal instinct, and by the blending of the two a human being was produced, – the union of the three fires in the causal vehicle.

---

[1] "*A Group-soul* is a collection of permanent Triads in a triple envelope of monadic essence. The permanent Triads are a reflection upon the lower planes of the spiritual Triads on the higher. This description is true of all group-souls functioning on the physical plane, but gives no idea of the extreme complexity of the subject." – From *A Study in Consciousness*, by Annie Besant.

(handwritten note: The three pyramids ... of Egypt.)

Man passes into the fifth kingdom through the trans-mutation of the discriminative faculty of mind, which – as in the animal's individualisation – brings about at a certain stage a spiritual individualisation which is the correspon-dence on higher levels to what transpired in Lemurian days. Therefore, we have:

> Instinct . . . The key from the animal into the human kingdom or from the third into the fourth kingdom.

> Manas . . . The key from the human into the spiritual kingdom, or from the fourth kingdom into the fifth kingdom.

A Treatise on Cosmic Fire, p. 335

In the third rootrace individualisation took place. It was an event which became possible through certain conditions and polar relationships, and because the scientific laws were un-derstood and the Knowers took advantage of a peculiar elec-trical condition to hasten the evolution of the race. It was electrical phenomena of a stupendous kind, and produced the "lights which ever burn." It was the result of the knowl-edge of natural law and its adaptation to opportunity.

That which is imprisoned must be loosed. So it will be in this rootrace, the fifth. Certain cosmic forces are at work and the full effect of their energy is not yet apparent. This incoming force, the Hierarchy will avail itself of in order to push forward the planetary plans. In every case the ef-fect of the phenomenon is felt in some one or other of the kingdoms beside the human. In the individualisation pe-riod, it is apparent that a tremendous stimulation took place in *the animal kingdom* – a stimulation which has persisted, and which has led to the phenomenon of "domestic animals" as we call them, and their relatively high stage of intelligence as compared to the wild animals.

A Treatise on Cosmic Fire, pp. 714-16

As we have seen, during the third rootrace, opportunity for the animal kingdom occurred and many individualised. In the fourth rootrace this cycle of opportunity ceased temporarily, and something happened which is analogous to what will occur in the fifth rootrace in connection with man, at the so-called "Judgment Day." In Atlantean days the lives which composed the third kingdom of nature were divided into two groups:

> A number of these lives were "passed," and the tide of life sweeps through them, permitting of their incarnating in animal form on earth, and their gradual evolution.
> The remainder were rejected, and as a group they became temporarily quiescent, and will not manifest in physical form until the next round.

In the fifth round, a corresponding division will take place in the fourth kingdom, and the lives in that kingdom will be subjected to an analogous test; some will be passed and will continue their evolution on this planet, while others will be rejected, and will go into temporary pralaya.

After the rejection in the fourth rootrace of three-fourths of the animal units, the remaining triads (or one-fourth) proceeded on their way holding the promise of opportunity for all in time, and the guarantee of their own attainment in the next round. Just as the human Monads, who are passed in the fifth round, will enter into the fifth kingdom, or respond to its vibration before the climax of the seventh, so the animal monads (if I may employ such a term) who were passed in this round will achieve individualisation during the fifth and enter the fourth kingdom. This will be brought about by the strong manasic impulse which will characterise the whole cycle of the fifth round, and will thus be effected normally and as the result of due evolutionary growth. An electrical stimulation of the nature of the occurrence in Lemurian days will not be required.

Ibid., pp. 461-62

[I]n the middle of the fourth root-race, the Atlantean, an event occurred which necessitated a change, or innovation in the Hierarchical method. Certain of its members were called away to higher work elsewhere in the solar system, and this brought in, through necessity, a number of highly evolved units of the human family. In order to enable others to take Their place, the lesser members of the Hierarchy were all moved up a step, leaving vacancies among the minor posts. Therefore three things were decided upon in the Council Chamber of the Lord of the World.

1. To close the door through which animal men passed into the human kingdom, permitting for a time no more Monads on the higher plane to appropriate bodies. This restricted the number of the fourth, or human kingdom, to its then limitation.

2. To open another door, and permit members of the human family who were willing to undergo the necessary discipline and to make the required stupendous effort, to enter the fifth or spiritual kingdom. In this way the ranks of the Hierarchy could be filled by the members of earth's humanity who qualified. This door is called the Portal of Initiation, and still remains open upon the same terms as laid down by the Lord of the World in Atlantean days. . . . The door between the human and animal kingdoms will again be opened during the next great cycle, or "round" as it is called in some books, but as this is several million years away from us at this time, we are not concerned with it.

Initiation, Human and Solar, pp. 33-4

Each kingdom is *positive* to the one next below it, and between them is found that period of manifestation which bridges the two, and connects the positive and the negative. The types of most intense rajas or activity in the mineral kingdom are found in those forms of life which are neither mineral nor vegetable but which bridge the two. Similarly in the vegetable kingdom, the rajas period is seen in fullest expression just before the activity becomes rhythmic and the vegetable merges in the animal. In the animal kingdom the same is seen in the animals which individualise, passing out of the group soul into separated identity. These types of activity must be regarded as constituting for the mineral, physical activity, for the vegetable, sentient activity, and for the animal, rudimentary mental activity.

A Treatise on Cosmic Fire, p. 1135

When the germ has developed to maturity the Mother aspect no longer has a place, and the Man occultly is freed or liberated. This idea runs through all manifestations, and the kingdoms of nature or the form (no matter what form it may be) nourish the germ of that which is the next step on in the evolutionary process, and are considered the Mother aspect. This aspect is eventually discarded and superseded. For example, the third kingdom, the animal, in the early stages nourishes and preserves the germ of that which will some day be a man; the personality is the preserver of that which will some day unfold into spiritual man.

a combination of
human { the animal soul &
the desire soul expressed

Ibid., p, 619

A careful study and a true analysis of the effect and work of the rays in connection with the animal kingdom is not possible. Yet it must be remembered that the roots of human psychology lie hidden in this expression of God. Humanity is an expression of two aspects of the soul, – the animal soul and the divine soul, – and these two, blended and fused in man, constitute the human soul. It is this fact that is the cause of man's special problems, and it is these two factors which involve him in the long struggle which eventuates in the liberation of the divine soul, through the sublimation of the animal soul. In these words lie much food for thought, "The twain shall be one". This work is begun in the animal kingdom, and constitutes its "secret", and hence the use of the word "transfusion" in this connection. Individualisation was the first result of this secret process. Its final consummating effect can be seen in the five stages of the initiatory process, leading to eventual transfiguration and liberation.

Esoteric Psychology I, p. 248

Only when the Self within, or the Ego in the causal body, is in control of his threefold personality can he occultly be permitted to be an alchemist of the fourth order, and work in connection with the transmutation of the animal monad into the human kingdom, with all the vast knowledge that is included in that idea.

A Treatise on Cosmic Fire, p. 487

DOMESTICATION AND THE SIX RAYS

This Science of Contact governs relations within our entire planetary life and includes, for instance, the rapport being established between humanity and the domesticated animals. These animals are to their own kingdom what the New Group of World Servers is to humanity. The New Group of World Servers is the linking bridge and the mode of communication between the Hierarchy (the fifth kingdom) and Humanity (the fourth kingdom) under the present divine Plan; the domesticated animals fulfil, therefore, an analogous function between Humanity (the fourth kingdom) and the animal kingdom (the third). These analogies are often fertile fields of illumination.

Telepathy and the Etheric Vehicle, p. 68

The animal kingdom has the quality of growing instinctual purpose which – in its highest form – works out as the domesticity of the more evolved animals, and their devotion to man. Behind the appearance of the animals is to be found a steady orientation towards understanding, and a consequent gravitation towards the forms of life which evidence that which they desire. Hence the influence of the fifth Ray of Concrete Knowledge, which pours through the human family upon the third kingdom in nature. Man is the initiating factor here, and to man is committed the task of leading the animal kingdom towards liberation – a liberation into the fourth kingdom, for that is the sphere of its next activity.

Esoteric Psychology I, p. 198

[I]t should be remembered that these ray forces express themselves as potently in other kingdoms in nature as they do in the human. For instance, one phase of the destructive aspects of first ray force has been the organised and scientific destruction of forms in the animal kingdom. This is the destroying force, as manipulated by man. Another phase of the same force (which can be noted in relation to the unfoldment of consciousness in subtle and powerful ways) can be seen in the effect which human beings have upon the domestic animals, hastening their evolution, and stimulating them into forms of advanced instinctual activity. I mention these two phases as illustration of the effect of first ray energy in the animal kingdom, as expressed through human activity.

The Destiny of the Nations, p. 14

The sixth ray is, as you know, very closely related to the animal kingdom and its effect there is to produce in the higher forms of animal life the quality and expression of domesticity, and the adaptability of the animal to human contact. The rays controlling the animal kingdom are the seventh, the third and the sixth. Hence you can easily see that the relation which exists between the higher animals and man is a ray relation and, therefore, useful under the evolutionary law and inevitable in its results.

Ibid., p. 123

The third ray is, in its turn, peculiarly related to the animal kingdom, producing the tendency to intelligent activity which we note in the higher domestic animals. The correspondence to radioactivity and to emanatory perfumes which we found in the mineral and vegetable kingdoms, we here call devotion, the characteristic of the attractive interplay between the domestic animals and man. Devotees of personalities might more rapidly transmute that devotion into its higher correspondence – love of principles – if they realised that they were only displaying an animal emanation.

Esoteric Psychology I, p. 45

The first point to be emphasized in connection with human responsibility in relation to the animals is that the animal world embodies two divine aspects, two divine principles, and two major rays are concerned with their expression or manifestation. These two aspects are found also in man, and it is along these two lines, which man shares in unison with the animals, that man's responsibility and work lie, and through the use of these two aspects of divine energy will he realise his task and carry it to completion. The same divine activity and the same divine innate intelligence are found in the form aspect of both kingdoms. They are inherent in matter itself. But this third Ray of Divine Intelligence functions more potently and influences more powerfully in the animal kingdom than in man. This is an item of information not hitherto given out.

The second ray is of course present in its form-building aspect, as herd instinct and as the basis of the sex relation among animal bodies. It is found performing a similar function among human beings, and along these two lines of energy will the points of contact be found and the opportunity to assume responsibility. Yet it should be noted that, in the last analysis, animals have more to give men than men have to give animals, where these particular powers and functions are concerned. In the human family another divine aspect is found functioning, which is that of the will, of directed purpose, of planned objective, and of intelligent design or plan. These qualities are inherent in man, and constitute an aspect of the divine mind not found actively present in the animal, as a rule. However, as the animal kingdom comes increasingly under human influence and the steady trend towards domesticity makes itself felt, we shall see emerging a measure of purposive objective; and one means towards this end is to be found in the turning of the animal's love and attention towards his master. In this illustration some of the responsibility of man to the animal world is expressed. The domestic animals have to be trained to participate in the action of applied will. This, man seems as yet to interpret as the will of the animal to love his master, but it is something deeper and more fundamental than the satisfying of man's love to be loved. The true and intelligent training of the wild animals, and their adaptation to the conditions of ordered living, are part of the divine process of integrating the Plan and of producing an ordered and harmonious expression of the divine intent. It is through the power of thought that man will eventually bridge the gap existing between the animal kingdom and man, and it must be done by man's directed, controlled thought, controlling and directing the animal consciousness. It is not done through the evocation of love, fear or pain. It is intended to be a purely mental process and a unique mental stimulation.

Esoteric Psychology I, pp. 254-56

In Atlantean days the purely physical relation was tempered by an astral or emotional relation, and the time came when some of the animals were swept within the orbit of human life and were tamed and cared for, and when the first of the domestic animals appeared. A new era began, wherein certain of the animals evoked affection from certain humans, and a new influence was brought to play upon this third kingdom in nature. This started during a cycle when the second ray and the sixth ray were both functioning simultaneously, and wherein their major and their lesser cycles coincided. This is a rare occurrence, and when it happens the guardians of the race seize the opportunity to produce major results or to inaugurate new moves whereby the divine Plan may be more rapidly developed. To offset the fear found in humanity as a whole (as far as the animal world was concerned), the opportunity was offered by the guardians of the race to bring men and animals into a closer relation, and because a cycle was present in which love and devotion were pouring upon, into and through all forms, a good deal of the fear present was offset. Since that time the number of the domestic animals has steadily increased. The relation between the two kingdoms is now dual–physical and emotional.

Esoteric Psychology I, p. 257

It will be clear that each of the kingdoms – elemental, mineral, vegetable, and animal as well as the human – is divided into seven primary types or rays, and as individualisation (i.e. the transition from the animal to the human kingdom) can take place at present only through association with man, it follows that there must stand at the head of the animal kingdom, on each ray, some species of animal susceptible to human influence through which such individualisation can take place. The elephant is said to stand at the head of the second ray type of animal, while the cat and dog occupy a similar position on the fourth and sixth rays respectively. We have had no information as to the others, with this exception, that the animals of the first ray are no longer in existence on earth.

Ibid., p. 164

In regard to the four minor Rays of Harmony, Concrete Science, Devotion and Ceremonial Order, their control exists in degrees on all the planes, but they have their particular emphasis in the evolution of the reincarnating ego in the three worlds at this time. These four Rays control, in a subtle and peculiar manner, the four kingdoms of nature – mineral, vegetable, animal and human – and at their merging into the three Rays of Aspect (the Activity Ray of the Mahachohan being the synthesiser of the lower four in our planetary scheme) have a correspondence with the merging of man (the product of the three kingdoms and the fourth) into the superman kingdom, the spiritual. The fourth Ray and the fourth Kingdom form a point of harmony for the lower three, and all four then pass into the major or upper three. This is worthy of our serious thought, and the analogy of the fourth plane will also be apparent. For this system, the buddhic plane, the human kingdom, and the fourth Ray of Harmony or Beauty or Synthesis, have a point of correspondence, just as the fourth rootrace is the one in which the synthesis is first observed – the door into the fifth kingdom of Spirit being then opened; the fourth rootrace also developed the astral capacity that made contact with the fourth or buddhic level possible.

In a subtle way too (I use the word subtle for lack of a better, meaning a statement of actuality that seems an illusion), the three minor Rays, Concrete Science, Devotion and Ceremonial Law, have each a connection with the three kingdoms of nature below the human, and with the three laws of the three lower worlds.

A Treatise on Cosmic Fire, pp. 588-89
The Ray of Concrete Science has a peculiar relationship

to the animal kingdom, in that it is the Ray that governs the merging of that kingdom into the human. The planet, Venus, in her fifth round, gave the impetus which produced the spark of mind in animal man – a fact well known. It is also the fifth Ray, and has an interesting connection with the fifth Law of Fixation. We might study, too, with profit, the analogy that can be seen between these factors and the fifth root-race, the race of peculiarly strong development of the concrete mind. The Law of Analogy always holds good.

A Treatise on Cosmic Fire, p. 590

Ray five will before long, as we have noted, make its power felt in the animal kingdom, and an ever closer relation will then be set up between men and animals.

Esoteric Psychology I, p. 247

The *animal kingdom* has the quality of growing instinctual purpose which – in its highest form – works out as the domesticity of the more evolved animals, and their devotion to man. Behind the appearance of the animals is to be found a steady orientation towards understanding, and a consequent gravitation towards the forms of life which evidence that which they desire. Hence the influence of the fifth Ray of Concrete Knowledge, which pours through the human family upon the third kingdom in nature. Man is the initiating factor here, and to man is committed the task of leading the animal kingdom towards liberation – a liberation into the fourth kingdom, for that is the sphere of its next activity.

Ibid., p. 198

I have little more to add to this teaching anent the animal kingdom and the rays, for – as said before – it profits not. Man's work is to raise the dead to life, to bring brotherhood into expression on the physical plane, and to transmit divine energy to a waiting world of forms. As the rays play their part with humanity and bring man forth into manifestation as he is in essence and reality, his work with the animal kingdom and with the other kingdoms will proceed steadily and inevitably. Scarcely knowing how or why, humanity will play its part in the work of building. The creative work will proceed and the Plan materialise. Man's work for the animal kingdom is to stimulate instinct until individualisation is possible.

Ibid., pp. 266-7

DEVAS

Forget not that the human evolution is but one of many, and that this is a period of crisis among the devas likewise. The call has gone forth for them to approach humanity, and with their heightened vibration and superior knowledge unite their forces with those of humanity, for the progression of the two evolutions. They have much to impart anent colour and sound, and their effect upon the etheric bodies of men and animals.

Esoteric Psychology I, p 123

The devas of water find for themselves the path of service in their great work of nourishing all the vegetable and animal life upon the planet; the goal for them is to enter into that higher group of devas which we call the gaseous or fire devas.

A Treatise on Cosmic Fire, p. 902

The *bird kingdom* is specifically allied to the deva evolution. It is the bridging kingdom between the purely deva evolution and two other manifestations of life.

First. Certain groups of devas who desire to pass into the human kingdom, having developed certain faculties, can do so via the bird kingdom, and certain devas who wish to get in communication with human beings can do so via the bird kingdom. This truth is hinted at in the Christian Bible and Christian religious representations by angels or devas being frequently represented as having wings. These cases are not many, as the usual method is for the devas gradually to work themselves towards individualisation through expansive feeling, but in the cases which do occur these devas pass several cycles in the bird kingdom, building in a response to a vibration which will ultimately swing them into the human family. In this way they become accustomed to the use of a gross form without the limitations, and impurities, which the animal kingdom engenders.

Second. Many devas pass out of the group of passive lives in the effort to become manipulating lives via the bird kingdom, and before becoming fairies, elves, gnomes, or other sprites, pass a certain number of cycles in the bird realm.

Why the two above events occur will not be apparent to the casual reader, nor will the true connection between the birds and the devas be accurately realised by the occult student unless he applies himself to the consideration of the "bird or swan out of time and space," and the place that birds play in the mysteries. Herein lies for him the clue. He must remember likewise the fact that every life of every degree, from a god to the most insignificant of the lesser devas, or builders, must at some time or another pass through the human family.

A Treatise on Cosmic Fire, pp. 895-96

The Agnichaitans; this is a term applied to the fiery lives, which are the sumtotal of the plane substance…., and also to the tiny essences which compose the fires of manifestation. As the nature of physical plane electricity is understood and studied, and its true condition realised, the reality of the existence of these agnichaitans will stand revealed.

Ibid., p. 904

These agnichaitans of the third subplane come particularly under the influence of Saturnian energy. They are the great fusers of substance, and it is in connection with them that the transmutation of metals becomes possible. They have a relationship to the mineral kingdom analogous to that which the watery devas have to the vegetable and animal. They are, as will be apparent, connected with the throat centre of a planetary Logos and of a solar Logos, and it is through their activity that the transmission of sound through the air becomes possible. It might surprise students and inventors could they but realise that the present rapid growth of wireless communication everywhere is due to the swinging into contact with the human vibration of a group of fiery deva lives hitherto uncontacted.

Ibid., p. 905

The devas who form the etheric doubles of all objects out of their own substance must also be considered. These builders are the sumtotal of all physical plane substance, and constitute the matter of the etheric levels of the physical plane. They exist, therefore, in four groups, and each group has a curious karmic relation to one of the four kingdoms in nature:

Group.	Plane.	Kingdom.
First	One	Human
Second	Two	Animal
Third	Three	Vegetable
Fourth	Four	Mineral

The substance of the highest physical form of a human being is therefore atomic. The Master's physical body is made of atomic matter, and when He wishes to materialise it on the dense physical plane, He forms a sheath of gaseous substance upon that atomic matter, perfect in its delineation of all the known physical traits. The substance of the highest form of animal body is that of the second ether, and herein is to be found a clue as to the relation between all sea and watery forms to the animal. The highest form of body possible for the vegetable form of life is that of the third ether. These facts will be demonstrated in the seventh round when the present three kingdoms of nature – the human, the animal, and the vegetable will objectively exist in etheric matter; that will be for them their densest manifestation. The mineral kingdom will find its highest manifestation in matter of the fourth ether, and this transmutation is already taking place, for all the radioactive substances now being discovered are literally becoming matter of the fourth ether.

A Treatise on Cosmic Fire, p. 935

One of the great errors into which the human family has fallen has been the endeavour to administer mineral drugs to man for medicinal purposes. It has resulted in a combination of deva substances which was never intended. The relation of man to the lower kingdoms, and particularly to the animal and mineral, has brought about a peculiar condition in the deva world and has tended to complicate deva evolution. The use of animal food (and the use of minerals as medicine in a lesser degree) has produced a commingling of deva substance, and of vibrations which are not attuned to each other. The vegetable kingdom is in a totally different situation, and part of its karma has lain in the providing of food for man; this has resulted in a needed transmutation of the life of that kingdom into the higher stage (the animal) which is its goal. The transmutation of vegetable life takes place necessarily on the physical plane. Hence its availability as food. The transmutation of the life of the animal into the human kingdom takes place on kama-manasic levels. Hence the non-availability, esoterically understood, of the animal as food for man. This is an argument for vegetarian living which needs due consideration.

Ibid., pp. 645-46

In dealing with the first group of forms, it must be noted that the pranic emanations given off by units of the animal and vegetable kingdom (after they have absorbed both solar and planetary prana) are naturally a combination of the two, and are transmitted by means of surface radiation, as in solar and planetary prana, to certain lesser groups of devas of a not very high order, who have a curious and intricate relationship to the group soul of the radiating animal or vegetable. This matter cannot be dealt with here. These devas are also of a violet hue, but of such a pale color as to be almost grey; they are in a transitional state, and merge with a puzzling confusion with groups of entities that are almost on the involutionary arc.

In dealing with the second group, the human form transmits the emanative radiations to a much higher grade of deva. These devas are of a more pronounced hue, and after due assimilation of the human radiation, they transmit it principally to the animal kingdom, thus demonstrating the close relationship between the two kingdoms. If the above explanation of the intricate inter-relation between the sun and the planets, between the planets and the evolving forms upon them, between the forms themselves in ever descending importance demonstrates nothing more than the exquisite interdependence of all existences, then much will have been achieved.

A Treatise on Cosmic Fire, pp. 95-6

GREAT INFORMING LIVES
AND THE CHAIN OF BEING

To that Great Life naught matters but humanity and its perfecting, because upon humanity depends the salvation of all the kingdoms in nature.

The Externalisation of the Hierarchy, p. 477

[T]he human kingdom (the fourth creative Hierarchy) was produced by a triple AUM sounded in a particular key by the three persons of the Trinity in unison, – God the Father, God the Son, and God the Holy Spirit, or Shiva, Vishnu, and Brahma. This sound is still going forth; the interplay and interblending of the many tiny notes of each human being produces a great united sound which can be heard in the high places and which, in its turn, is having a definite effect upon the animal kingdom. It is one of the factors which produces animal forms, both for human and animal occupation, for it must ever be remembered that man links the animal and the divine.

Initiation, Human and Solar, p. 152

[I]n the flow of force from a particular constellation, outside our system altogether, through a particular planetary scheme, and thus through the astral body of a planetary Logos, a condition was brought about which produced the appearance of the third kingdom in nature, the sentient conscious animal kingdom.

A Treatise on Cosmic Fire, p. 665

Varuna, the Lord of the astral plane, has achieved a more unified conscious control than His brothers of the mental and physical planes…. We may justly ask why, if this is so, it should apparently manifest so disastrously in connection with man? There are several reasons for this, one being … that he has a peculiar link with the Ruler of the animal kingdom, and as the human being has not yet dissociated himself from, nor learnt to control, his animal nature, he too comes under the influence of this tremendous force.

Ibid., pp. 660-61

[T]he sumtotal of human and deva units upon a planet make the *body vital* of a planetary Logos, whilst the sumtotal of lesser lives upon a planet (from the material bodies of men or devas down to the other kingdoms of nature) form His body corporeal, and are divisible into two types of such lives:

a.   Those on the evolutionary arc, such as in the animal kingdom.
b.   Those on the involutionary arc …

Ibid., pp. 301-02

The "prisoners of the planet" fall into two categories:

1. Those lives which act under the influence of a conscious purpose, and who "limit the life that is in them" for a time. They consciously take form, knowing the end from the beginning. These Beings in their turn fall into three main groups.

    a. The Being Who is the life of our planet, the One in Whom we live and move and have our being. This being, or sum total of organised lives is sometimes called the planetary Logos sometimes the Ancient of Days, sometimes God, and sometimes the One Life.

    b. Those lives who constitute the Principle of Limitation in a kingdom of nature. The Life that is, for instance, expressing itself through the medium of the animal kingdom is a self-conscious intelligent entity, working in full awareness of intent and objective, and limiting his sphere of activity in order to provide due opportunity and expression for the myriad lives that find their life and being and sustenance in him. See you how the law of sacrifice runs throughout creation.

    c. The sons of mind, human souls, solar Angels, the divine sons of God who in full self-consciousness work out certain well seen ends through the medium of the human family.

2. Those lives who are limited in form because they are not self-conscious but are unconscious constituent parts of a greater form. They have not yet evolved to the point where they are self-conscious entities.

A Treatise on White Magic, pp. 530-31

In the fourth rootrace the "door" (as it is called) between the two kingdoms became closed, and no more of the animal kingdom passed into the human. Their cycle temporarily ended and – to express it in terms of fire or of electrical phenomena – the animal kingdom and the human became positive to each other, and repulsion instead of attraction supervened. All this was brought about by the swinging into power of a profoundly long cycle of the fifth Ray. This was necessitated by the need of man to develop along the manasic line, and resulted in a period of repulsion of the animal units, leaving their consciousness to be stimulated on astral lines.

Owing to this repulsion, we have one reason (and one of the least fundamental) for the destructive war and the long cycle of cruelty that has been waged between man and the animals. It can be evidenced in the terror of man in connection with wild animals of the jungles and the deserts, and in the terrible toll of life that such animals have exacted during the centuries. This must not be forgotten. For thousands of years, wild animals have – specially before the coming in of firearms – destroyed the defenseless, and during those years, had statistics been taken, the numbers of human beings killed would reach a stupendous figure. Now, in this age, the balancing is taking place and in the slaughter of animals equilibrium is being reached. I do not refer to the wanton cruelties practised under the name of science, nor to certain practices which take place under religious guise in different lands. The source of these enormities must be sought for elsewhere. It is hidden in the karma of that Being, Who for a period – during the moon chain – held office as the Entity Who is the informing evolutionary Life of the animal kingdom. This is a point of view needing careful pondering. Each of the kingdoms of nature is the expression of a Life or Being; man, for instance, being the expression of one or other of the Heavenly Men; the sumtotal of humanity (the fourth Hierarchy) being found, with the deva evolution, as the centres of the solar Logos. The animal kingdom likewise is the expression of the life of a Being Who is a part of the body of the Logos or of the planetary Logos, but not a centre of conscious energy. (A correspondence is found in the human body, which has its seven centres of force or energy, but also other organs upon which objective manifestation depends in lesser degree.) Such an Entity finds expression through the animal kingdom, of which He is the informing Soul, and He has definite place in the planetary or logoic body. This is a hint which has hitherto not been exoteric and is to be commended to the consideration of students. I would add that some of the tragedies underlying existence at this time are karmically incident upon temporarily faulty relations between an entity who dominated at one period of the third or moon-chain, and the one holding analogous position in this the fourth or earth chain. This latter is the sumtotal of the lowest human principle, if we count the dense physical or animal body of man as a principle. In their lack of agreement lies the clue to the cruelties practised on animals by man.

A Treatise on Cosmic Fire, pp. 459-61

Since the great division in the fourth rootrace, the animal kingdom has been primarily occupied with the stimulation and development of kama. This is the basis of the endeavour being made by the Brotherhood *by the aid of man* to fan the emotional instinct (or the embryo love aspect) through the segregating of the domestic animals, and the consequent play made upon the third spirilla in the animal atoms by human magnetism or radiatory energy. The sumtotal of the domestic animals – the animal units brought into closest connection with man – form the heart centre in the body of that great Entity Who is the life of the animal kingdom. From the heart flow all the influences which will eventually permeate the entire body. These units are those which will be finally separated from the group soul at the reopening of the door into the human kingdom in the next round.

A Treatise on Cosmic Fire, p. 462

The work of the Aryan Adepts is to impress upon the world consciousness that God is Will. To do this for the human family, They work with the intellect so as to bring it into control, to subordinate other forms to the mind and through the mind to reveal to man the vision of what is and what will be. Man is therefore brought into line with the esoteric head centre of the one Life. In the animal kingdom, through the development of sentiency and its allied unfoldment through pain, They are bringing those types of forms into line with the heart centre in Nature. This is a phrase conveying a truth which cannot be more clearly expressed until man has become more inclusive

in his consciousness. Through colour in the vegetable Kingdom those forms of divine manifestation are also brought
into vibratory contact with that centre of force in Nature
which is analogous to the throat centre in man.

In using these words I refer primarily to the Life which
is expressing itself through our planet, to our planetary
Logos, but the idea can (needless to say) be progressed to
include the great Life of which our planetary Logos is but
a reflection and an expression. Man, the brain of nature; the
animals, the expression of the heart; the vegetable world,
the expression of the creative force or of the throat centre;
these three kingdoms in nature forming, in a peculiar manner, correspondences to the three higher centres in man, as
the three kingdoms on the involutionary arc correspond to
the three lower centres, and the mineral kingdom – abstruse
as the idea may seem to those of you who have not the consciousness of the life-aspect – corresponding to the solar
plexus, the great clearing house between that which is
above and that which is below.

These analogies change as time progresses. In
Lemurian days, viewing it as a kingdom in nature, humanity expressed the solar plexus aspect, whilst the animal kingdom stood for the sacral centre, and the centre
at the base of the spine was symbolised by the vegetable
kingdom. In the middle of the Atlantean period, when
certain great changes and experiments were wrought, a
shift in the entire process took place; certain egos came
in, as you know, as related in *The Secret Doctrine* and in
A Treatise on Cosmic Fire, and a tremendous stepping

forward became possible through their efforts. The chitta or mind-stuff became more vibrant and now we have the period of its intensest activity in the concrete sense.

A Treatise on White Magic, pp. 359-61

The secret of the *reptile kingdom* is one of the mysteries of the second round, and there is a profound significance connected with the expression "the serpents of wisdom" which is applied to all adepts of the good law. The reptile kingdom has an interesting place in all mythologies, and all ancient forms of truth impartation, and this for no arbitrary reason. It is not possible to enlarge upon the underlying truth which is hidden in the karmic history of our planetary Logos, and is revealed as part of the teaching given to initiates of the second degree.

The second great life impulse, or life wave, initiated by our planetary Logos, when brought in conjunction with the first, was the basis of that activity which we call evolutionary energy; it resulted in a gradual unrolling, or revelation, of the divine form. The heavenly serpent manifested, being produced out of the egg, and began its convolutions, gaining in strength and majesty, and producing through its immense fecundity millions of lesser "serpents." The reptile kingdom is the most important part of the animal kingdom in certain aspects, if such an apparently contradictory statement can be made. For all animal life can be seen passing through it during the prenatal stage, or returning to it when the form is in advanced decomposition. The connection is not purely a physical one, but it is also psychic. When the real nature and method of the kundalini, or serpent fire, is known, this relation will be better understood, and the history of the second round assume a new importance.

A Treatise on Cosmic Fire, pp. 892-93

The lunar Pitris, and lesser builders from the systemic point of view find their fullest expression in the animal kingdom. When they, as the initiatory impulse, had produced animal man they had performed their prime function, and just as (on a smaller scale and in connection with only one of the Heavenly Men) the moon is a dying and decadent world, so on a systemic scale and therefore covering a vast period of time, the work of the lunar Pitris is slowly coming to a conclusion as the power of the third kingdom, the animal, over the human is being superseded by spiritual power; the systemic correspondence to lunar pitric activity will occultly die out.

Ibid., pp. 617-18

The *animal kingdom* is responsive to a type of energy which is neither fire nor water but is a combination of the two. They are also the first of the kingdoms on the physical plane to be responsive to *sound,* or to the energy emanating from that which we call noise. This is an occult fact worthy of close attention. The energy emanating from the Entity Who is the informing Life of the third kingdom in nature has five channels of approach, that is five centres. That animating the fourth kingdom has seven, for the mind and the intuition are added. In the second kingdom there are three centres, but their manifestation is so obscure as to seem practically nonexistent to the human mind. In the first or mineral kingdom, the avenue of approach is limited to one centre. It will be observed, therefore, that the stimulation of magnetic energy proceeds from what might be regarded as jumps, 1-3-5-7. Each kingdom starts with a specific equipment, and during the process of evolution within the kingdom adds to it so that the liberated life enters the next kingdom with its old equipment plus one. . . .

The atom becomes responsive to form energy or to that which surrounds it. It becomes conscious and then becomes responsive to the force of the *kingdom* in which it is a part. It gradually becomes responsive to stronger influences or to the force emanating from the Entity Who is the life of that kingdom.

Finally, the atom becomes conscious of planetary energy, or responsive to the Heavenly Man Himself. It then transcends the kingdom in which it has been, and is elevated into another kingdom in which the cycle is again repeated.

This can all be expressed in terms of consciousness but in this section we will limit the thought simply to that of energy. In summation it might be said that:

1. The planetary Logos has seven centres, as has man.
2. The informing Life of the animal kingdom has five centres, and the animal kingdom has five prototypes on the archetypal plane, whereas man has seven prototypes.

A Treatise on Cosmic Fire, pp. 1072-73

Every thought form comes under the law of Karma through the effect it produces. At this stage in the history of the system – that vast transitional stage between dense physical life and existence in the logoic etheric body – it is not easy for us to differentiate between those thought forms which are effects and those which are causes. It should be remembered here that *only cosmic and solar lords formulate thoughts.* The lunar Lords and all lesser intelligences do not do so. Therefore, the two above mentioned groups come under karmic law. They only are self-conscious, and therefore responsible. Where self-consciousness is not, there is no responsibility. Hence animals are not held to be responsible, and though they suffer on the physical plane and in their physical vehicles, on the subtler planes they are freed from karma, for they have neither memory nor anticipation; they lack the correlating faculty and as the spark of mind is missing, they are held free from the law of retribution, except where the physical body is concerned. The reason for the suffering in the animal kingdom is hidden in the mystery of the sin of the mindless,* and in that terrible period

---

* *The sin of the Mindless.* See S. D., II, 195, 201. This sin has to do with the period of the Separation of the Sexes in the early third rootrace, the Lemurian. The same historical fact is hinted at also in the Bible in Genesis VI, 2:4.

"They (the sexes) had already separated before the ray of divine reason had enlightened the dark region of their hitherto slumbering minds, and had *sinned.* That is to say, they had committed evil unconsciously by producing an effect which was unnatural." See also S. D., II, 721, 728.

spoken of in the *Secret Doctrine*, which resulted in abortions and distortions of all kinds. Had this period not occurred, and this particular type of "miscarriage of purpose" not taken place, we should not have had the fearful karmic relationship which now exists between the third and the fourth kingdom.

A Treatise on Cosmic Fire, pp. 562-63

The average Christian confuses the Law of Rebirth with what he calls "the transmigration of souls" and frequently believes that the Law of Rebirth signifies the passing of human beings into the bodies of animals or of lower forms of life. Such is by no means the case. As the life of God progresses onwards through form after form, that life in the sub-human kingdoms of nature proceeds progressively from mineral forms into vegetable forms, and from these vegetable forms into animal forms; from the animal form stage, the life of God passes into the human kingdom, and becomes subject to the Law of Rebirth and not the law of Transmigration. To those who know something of the Law of Rebirth or of Reincarnation, the mistake seems ridiculous.

The Reappearance of the Christ, pp. 115-16

The fourth Creative Hierarchy, viewed as a unit functioning on this planet (and leaving out of consideration its manifestation in other schemes) works in a magnetic manner, and in a stimulative capacity upon the animal kingdom, the force of its vibration pouring on to the *astral bodies* of the animals, and producing response. This awakens to a more effective apprehension all the units of the animal kingdom. Hence it can be seen how close is the interplay, and the interdependence, and how closely united all these greater and lesser lives are with each other. Growth and development in one part of the body logoic produces a corresponding advance in the whole. No man, for instance, can make definite and specialised progress without his brother benefiting, – this benefiting taking the form of:

The increase of the total consciousness of the group.
The stimulation of units in the group.
The group magnetism producing increased healing or blending effects upon allied groups.

In this thought lies, for the servant of the Master, incentive to effort; no man who strives for mastery, who struggles to attain, and who aims at expansion of consciousness but is having some effect – in ever widening spirals – upon all whom he contacts, devas, men, and animals. That he knows it not, and that he may be totally unaware of the subtle stimulating emanation which proceeds from him may be true, but nevertheless the law works.

A Treatise on Cosmic Fire, pp. 464-65

EVOLUTIONARY DEVELOPMENTS
AND THE SEVENTH RAY

One of the inevitable effects of seventh ray energy will be to relate and weld into a closer synthesis the four kingdoms in nature. This must be done as preparatory to the long fore-ordained work of humanity which is to be the distributing agency for spiritual energy to the three subhuman kingdoms. This is the major task of service which the fourth kingdom, through its incarnating souls, has undertaken. The radiation from the fourth kingdom will some day be so potent and far-reaching that its effects will permeate down into the very depths of the created phenomenal world, even into the mineral kingdom. Then we shall see the results to which the great initiate, Paul, refers when he speaks of the whole creation waiting for the manifestation of the Sons of God. That manifestation is that of radiating glory and power and love.

Incidentally I might point out here that the seventh ray influence will have three definite effects upon the fourth and third kingdoms in nature. These are as follows:

1. All animal bodies will be steadily refined and in the case of humanity consciously refined, and so brought to a higher and more specialised state of development. . . .

2. The relation between the human and the animal kingdoms will become increasingly close. The service of the animal to man is well recognised and of ceaseless expression. The service of man to the animals is not yet understood though some steps in the right direction are being taken. There must eventually be a close synthesis and sympathetic coordination between them and when this is the case some very extraordinary occurrences of animal mediumship under human inspiration will take place. By means of this, the intelligent factor in the animal (of which instinct is the embryonic manifestation) will be rapidly developed and this is one of the outstanding results of the intended human-animal relationship.

3. There will be, as a consequence of this quickened evolution, the rapid destruction of certain types of animal bodies. Very low grade human bodies will disappear, causing a general shift in the racial types towards a higher standard. Many species of animals will also die out and are today disappearing, and hence the increasing emphasis upon the preservation of animals and the establishing of game preserves.

The Destiny of the Nations, pp. 124-25

Much of profound interest is on its way as a result of this seventh ray activity. For one thing, though the animal kingdom reacts but little to this type of influence, yet there are going to be very definite results within the soul of the animal form. The door of individualisation or of entrance into the human kingdom has been closed since Atlantean times, but under the new influence it will be partially opened; it will be set ajar, so that a few animals will respond to soul stimulation and discover that their rightful place is on the human side of the dividing door. Part of the reorganisation which will go on as a result of the seventh ray activity will concern the relation of humanity to the animal kingdom and the establishing of better and of closer relations. This will lead men to take advantage of another effect of the seventh ray, which is its power to refine the matter out of which the forms are built. The animal body of man has received much scientific attention during the past one hundred years, and medicine and surgery have reached great heights of achievement. The framework of man, his body, and its internal systems (with their diverse rituals) are now understood as never before, and this has been the result of the incoming ray force with its power to apply knowledge to the magical work. When this knowledge is applied intensively to the animal world much new and interesting data will be discovered; when the differences between the physical bodies of the animals and those of humanity have been more closely investigated there will appear a new and very fruitful field of study. These differences are largely in the realm of the nervous systems; not enough attention has been paid for instance to the fact that the brain of the animal is really in the region of the solar plexus, whilst the human brain, the controlling agent, is in the head, and works through the medium of the spinal column. When scientists know exactly why the animal does not use the brain in the head as does man, they will arrive at a fuller knowledge of the law governing cycles.

Esoteric Psychology I, pp. 371-72

The third effect of the coming in of this ray [seventh] is one that may at first repel – it will cause a great destruction in the animal kingdom. During the next few hundred years many of the old animal forms will die out and become extinct. To supply the wants of man, through disease, and through causes latent in the animal kingdom itself, much destruction will be brought about. It must ever be borne in mind that a building force is likewise a destroying one, and new forms for the animal evolution are, at this time, one of the recognized needs. The immense slaughter in America is part of the working out of the plan. The inner life or fire which animates the animal groups, and which is the life expression of an Entity, will, under this seventh influence, blaze up and burn out the old, and permit the escape of the life, to newer and better forms.

A Treatise on Cosmic Fire, p. 465

Humanity is macrocosmic in relation to the sub-human states of consciousness, and this H. P. B. has well pointed out. The effect upon these lesser and more material states is primarily four-fold.

1. The stimulating of the spiritual aspect, expressing itself as the soul in all forms, such as the form of a

mineral, a flower, or an animal. The positive aspect of energy in all these forms will wax stronger, producing radiation, for instance, increasingly in the mineral kingdom. In this lies a hint of the nature of the process that will set a term to our own planetary existence and eventually, to our solar system.

In the animal kingdom the effect will be the elimination of pain and suffering and a return to the ideal conditions of the Garden of Eden. When man functions as a soul, he heals; he stimulates and vitalizes; he transmits the spiritual forces of the universe, and all harmful emanations and all destructive forces find in the human kingdom a barrier. Evil and its effects are largely dependent upon humanity for a functioning channel. Humanity's function is to transmit and handle force. This is done in the early and ignorant stages destructively and with harmful results. Later when acting under the influence of the soul, force is rightly and wisely handled and good eventuates. True indeed it is that "the whole creation travaileth in pain until now, waiting for the manifestation of the sons of God."

2. The bringing of light. Humanity is the planetary light bearer, transmitting the light of knowledge, of wisdom, and of understanding, and this in the esoteric sense. These three aspects of light carry three aspects of soul energy to the soul in all forms, through the medium of the anima mundi, the world soul. Physically speaking, this can be realized if we can appreciate the difference between

our planetary illumination today and that of five hundred years ago – our brilliantly lit cities, our rural districts, shining through the night with their lighted streets and homes; our airways, outlined with their search-lights and fields of blazing globes; our oceans, dotted with their lighted ships, and increasingly our lighted airships will be seen, darting through the skies.

These are but the result of man's growing illumination. His knowledge aspect of light has brought this into being. Who shall say what will eventuate when the wisdom aspect predominates? When these are welded by understanding, the soul will control in the three worlds and in all kingdoms of nature.

3. The transmission of energy. The clue to the significance of this can be grasped as a concept, though as yet it will fail of comprehension, in the realization that the human kingdom acts upon and affects the three sub-human kingdoms. The downpouring spiritual Triangle and the upraising matter Triangle meet point to point in humanity when the point of balance can be found. In man's achievement and spiritualization is the hope of the world. Mankind itself is the world Saviour, of which all world Saviours have been but the symbol and the guarantee.

4. The blending of the deva or angel evolution and the human.

A Treatise on White Magic, pp. 99-100

The work of the devas in connection with the animal and the vegetable kingdoms will be likewise recognised, and much that is now possible through ignorance will become impossible and obsolete. The time will come, when the attitude of man to the animal kingdom will be revolutionised, and the slaughter, ill-treatment, and that form of cruelty called "sport," will be done away with.

A Treatise on Cosmic Fire, p. 475

The mental power of humanity will, in the last analysis, be the controlling factor, and through its means the three sub-human kingdoms will be brought under the control of man. This has been happening with great rapidity in the mineral kingdom and in the vegetable kingdom. It is not yet accomplished where the animal kingdom is concerned, but the process is rapidly going forward. Not much progress will be made during the incoming seventh ray cycle, though as law and order and rhythm are imposed upon the planet, and as chaos gives place to organisation, we shall see those areas on the planet wherein the animals still rule increasingly lessened, and certain species will die out unless they are preserved in sanctuaries.

Esoteric Psychology I, pp. 257-58

If the societies and organisations, connected with the spiritualistic movement and the psychical research groups, would seek for and find the natural sensitives (and not the trance mediums) and those who are naturally clair-audient and clair-voyant and would study their disclosures, their words, their reactions and their modes of working they would discover much about some of the natural and normal powers of man – powers which have been in abeyance during the period wherein mind development has been the objective and which humanity shares with two great groups of lives – the Members of the Hierarchy and the animal kingdom. Ponder on this.

The Destiny of the Nations, pp. 44-5

The next step ahead for science . . . should concern the potential force of the atom itself, and its harnessing for the use of man. This will let loose upon earth a stupendous amount of energy. Nevertheless, it is only when the third factor is comprehended, and science admits the agency of mental fire as embodied in certain groups of devas, that the force of energy that is triple, and yet one in the three worlds, will become available for the helping of man. This lies as yet far ahead, and will only become possible towards the end of this round; and these potent forces will not be fully utilised, nor fully known till the middle of the next round. At that time, much energy will become available through the removal of all that obstructs. This is effected, in relation to man, at the Judgment separation, but it will produce results in the other kingdoms of nature also. A portion of the animal kingdom will enter into a temporary obscuration, thus releasing energy for the use of the remaining percentage, and producing results such as are hinted at by the prophet of Israel when he speaks of "the wolf lying down with the lamb"; his comment "a little child shall lead them" is largely the esoteric enunciation of the fact that three fifths of the human family will stand upon the Path 'a little child' being the name applied to probationers and disciples. In the vegetable and mineral kingdoms a corresponding demonstration will ensue, but of such a nature as to be too obscure for our comprehension.

A Treatise on Cosmic Fire, pp. 492-93

When the rate of the vibration of a larger percentage of the race has reached a certain measure, and when the colour aspect of the co-ordinated auras of the groups is of a certain tone, they [very highly developed souls] will return, and bring to the earth much of value past your realisation.

[T]he rhythmic effect on even the two kingdoms beneath the human will be objectively demonstrable. It was no idle boast of the prophet of Israel when he said "The leopard shall lie down with the lamb" or that "the desert shall blossom like a rose". It will be brought about by the domination of certain vibrations and the bringing in of certain colours veiling certain virtues or influences.

Letters on Occult Meditation, pp. 236-37

All the creative functions of the vegetable, animal, and human family, viewing them as a whole, are as yet purely physical, and based on lower desire. The desire of the Logos for physical incarnation is as yet the dominant note. Later His desire for that will be less and will become transmuted into desire for creation on mental levels only. This is what brings the Destroyer aspect into activity, leading to eventual obscuration, and the physical "death" of the solar system. Indication that this aspect is coming into power will be seen when two great events transpire:

a.   The ability of man consciously to create on mental levels, and the consequent transmutation of his lower sex impulses into higher.

b.   The mental vitalisation of another large section of the animal kingdom.

A Treatise on Cosmic Fire, pp. 557-58

The sex aspect – as at present expressing itself – and the whole process of reproduction is one which man shares with the animal kingdom, and is based upon his animal instincts, and his dense physical nature, which is not a principle. When he is totally emancipated from the animal kingdom, and the third and fourth kingdoms stand distinct from each other, then the sex nature, and the organs of reproduction will be viewed by the average man in a very different manner than at present. Creation will eventually be *the result of thought impulses and not desire impulses*; . . . This stage will be entered upon when the functions of the etheric body are scientifically grasped and understood and the laws of creative thought are a matter of public knowledge and discussion; it will coincide with a period wherein the animal kingdom will again be under manasic impression, and individualisation will again be permitted.

Ibid., p. 559

In the next root race, ray five will commence to pour its power into the animal kingdom, gradually stimulating the instinctual mind of the animal until it vibrates to the ray of the intellect, of knowledge. This will bring about an organising of the animal brain, and the transfer of the power of the solar plexus centre to the head centre, and consequently a shift in the animal polarisation and an added activity of the brain in the head.

Esoteric Psychology I, p. 243

The planetary centre which corresponds to the one at the base of the spine in the human being will not be awakened until the seventh root-race and that only when right relationship is established between the planetary sacral centre (which is related to the third kingdom in nature, the animal kingdom) and the planetary throat centre, functioning properly and in unison.

Esoteric Astrology, p. 454

Six of the Masters, as yet quite unknown to the average occult student by name, have already sought physical incarnation – one in India, another in England, two in northern America, and one in central Europe, whilst another has made a great sacrifice, and taken a Russian body in the desire to act as a peace centre in that distracted land. Certain initiates of the third Initiation have taken feminine bodies, – one in India will in due time do much toward the emancipation of the women of India, whilst another has a peculiar work to do in connection with the animal kingdom which likewise is awaiting the day of His appearing.

A Treatise on Cosmic Fire, p. 758

As the moon becomes small through the process of disintegration, its effect upon the Earth will be correspondingly lessened, and this stage will be paralleled by a consequent greater freedom from evil impulse of the sons of men. Better conditions among the animals will be another result above all else, and the dying out of that which is noxious in the animal kingdom.

Ibid., p. 795

When, however, the consciousness of man is opened up in such a manner that it can register that which is proceeding and taking place in the three lower kingdoms in nature, then further light and information will be given. This will take place in a period of human history when Libra is dominant and the three divine aspects of the third Person of the Trinity, the Holy Spirit, the Creator – law, sex and money – will give the clue to the three lower kingdoms. Law, natural law (the externalisation of the subjective spiritual law) will give the clue to the animal kingdom. . . .

Esoteric Astrology, p. 244-245

The blue ray of devotion passes now into the violet of what we term the ceremonial ray. What do these words mean? Simply that the great Musician of the universe is moving the keys, is sounding another note and thus bringing in another turn of the wheel, and swinging into the arc of manifestation the ray of violet, the great note G. These rays bring with them – in every kingdom in nature – all that is attuned to them: Human beings, devas of order high or low, elementals of a desirable or undesirable nature, flowers, fruits, and vegetable life of a certain kind, and animals and forms of varying species. It is the passing out of a ray that signals the ultimate extinction of some particular form, some type of animal life, and leads to some vegetable aspect coming to an end.

Esoteric Psychology I, pp. 121-22

Animals and human beings and the Rays. We will now take up two points and study the effect of the incoming force on the human and animal kingdoms.

These points are of profound interest to the occult student for two reasons. The topic we have now to consider is the effect of the incoming seventh Ray during the coming centuries upon the animal kingdom and the deva evolution. The profundity of the interest lies in the fact that in the one case we are dealing with the evolution immediately behind the human and from which man is not as yet wholly emancipated, and in the other we are concerning ourselves with a paralleling evolution, and one that is of vast importance in the scheme of things. Let us take up first this *seventh Ray and its effect upon the animal kingdom.*

Practically little is known to man concerning this kingdom of nature, save what science has vouchsafed anent the physical organisms, and a few occult statements which have been given out at various times; the development of the animal consciousness and its immediate future is as yet but little understood.

The most important of the occult facts concerning this third kingdom as they relate to our present subject, may be enumerated as follows:

1. The animal kingdom holds the same relation to the human kingdom as the dense physical body does to the seven principles and still finds its connecting link with man through the close correspondence between their bodies of objectivity.

2. The animal kingdom is the third of the kingdoms and is (from the esoteric point of view and as regards its relation to mankind) the mother aspect, prior to the overshadowing by the Holy Spirit, the manas aspect. Think out this resemblance, and trace the analogy between the cosmic mother, the systemic mother, and the same mother aspect as seen in the animal kingdom as a basis for the evolution of man.

Each of the kingdoms of nature acts as the mother to the succeeding one in the evolutionary process. Any group, which may be under consideration, should in due course of evolution give birth to offspring, who will – in themselves – embody some ideal, and who receive their objective forms on some plane from the earlier group. From the third kingdom springs the fourth, and from this fourth will emerge the fifth, each receiving

a. Germ protection,
b. Form,
c. Gradual development,
d. Nourishment,

until in each case the human child, or the Christ child, is brought to the birth. This is a very occult truth, and though the facts have been recognised and taught anent the fourth and fifth kingdoms, the work and place of the animal has not received its due recognition.

A Treatise on Cosmic Fire, pp. 457-58

Let us now consider the immediate present, and the advent of this seventh ray of ceremonial magic. The effect upon the animal kingdom of the force of this ray will be far less than upon the human, for it is not yet ready to respond to the vibration of this planetary Logos, and will not be until the sixth round when His influence will bring about great events. Nevertheless, certain effects might here be noticed.

Owing to the increased activity of the deva evolution, and specially of the devas of the ethers, the lesser builders will be stimulated to build, with greater facility, bodies of a more responsive nature, and the etheric bodies of both men and animals and also their responsiveness to force or prana will be more adequate. During the sixth subrace, disease as we know it in both kingdoms will be materially lessened owing to the pranic response of the etheric bodies. This will likewise bring about changes in the dense physical body and the bodies of both men and animals will be smaller, more refined, more finely attuned to vibration, and consequently more fitted to express essential purpose.

Owing to the recognition by man of the value of mantrams, and his gradual comprehension of the true ceremonial of evolution, coupled with the use of sound and colour, the animal kingdom will be better understood, and better trained, considered and utilised. Indications of this already can be seen; for instance, in all our current magazines at this time, stories which deal with the psychology of animals, and with their mental attitude to man, are constantly appearing, and by the means of these and through the force of the incoming Ray, man may (if he cares to do so) come to a much wider sympathy with his brothers of less degree. Thus by the turning by man of his thought force upon the animals, stimulation of their latent mentality will ensue, leading in due course of time to the crisis in the next round. More attention should be paid by occult students to the effect of the consciousness of one group upon another group, and the advancement of the lesser, by the means of the stimulating power of the greater, should be studied.

A Treatise on Cosmic Fire, pp. 462-63

When perfection has been achieved, the Shamballa energy of will, power and purpose will pour freely through the head centre, the love-wisdom energies of the Hierarchy will flow through the heart centre, and the energy of humanity will focus through the throat centre, with the ajna centre acting as the agent of all three. Then will take place a new activity on the part of mankind. It is the task of relating the three superhuman kingdoms to the three subhuman kingdoms, and thus establishing the new heavens and the new earth. Then humanity will have reached the summit of its evolutionary goal on this Earth.

Esoteric Healing, p. 154

ADDENDA

THE ANIMAL KINGDOM

Influences . . . The third Ray of Active Intelligence or of Adaptability is potent in this kingdom and will express itself increasingly as time goes on, until it can best be described as "animal one-pointedness." Then, at this point and cyclically, the sixth Ray of Devotion or Idealism can make its pressure felt as the urge towards a goal, and thus produce a relation to man which makes of him the desired goal. This is to be seen through the medium of the tamed, the trained and the domestic animals.

Results . . . . . In the one case we find the third ray producing the emergence of instinct, which in its turn creates and uses that marvellous response apparatus we call the nervous system, the brain, and the five senses which lie behind and which are responsible for them as a whole. It should be noted that, wide as we may regard the difference between man and the animals, it is really a much closer relation than that existing between the animal and the vegetable. In the case of the sixth ray, we have the appearance of the power to be domesticated and trained, which is, in the last analysis, the power to love, to serve and to emerge from the herd into the group. Ponder on the words of this last paradoxical statement.

Process. . . . . . This is called concretisation. In this kingdom we have for the first time a true organisation of the etheric body into what are called by the esotericist "the true nerves and the sensory centres." Plants also have nerves, but they have in them nothing of the same intricacy of relation and of plexus as we find in the human being and in the animal. Both kingdoms share the same general grouping of nerves, of force centres and channels, with a spinal column and a brain. This organisation of a sensitive response apparatus constitutes, in reality, the densification of the subtle etheric body.

Secret ...... This is called transfusion, which is a very inadequate word to express the early blending, in the animal, of the psychological factors which lead to the process of individualisation. It is a process of lifegiving, of intelligent integration and of psychological unfoldment, to meet emergency.

Purpose ..... This is called experimentation. Here we come to a great mystery, and one that is peculiar to our planet. In many esoteric books it has been stated and hinted that there has been a mistake, or a serious error, on the part of God Himself, of our planetary Logos, and that this mistake has involved our planet and all that it contains in the visible misery, chaos and suffering. Shall we say that there has been no mistake, but simply a great experiment, of the success or failure of which it is not yet possible to judge? The objective of the experiment might be stated as follows: It is the intent of the planetary Logos to bring about a psychological condition which can best be described as one of "divine lucidity". The work of the psyche, and the goal of the true psychology, is to see life clearly, as it is, and with all that is involved. This does not mean conditions and environment, but Life. This process was begun in the animal kingdom, and will be consummated in the human. These are described in the *Old Commentary* as "the two eyes of Deity, both blind at first, but which later see, though the right eye sees more clearly than the left". The first dim indication of this tendency towards lucidity is seen in the faculty of the plant to turn towards the sun. It is practically non-existent in the mineral kingdom.

Divisions . . . . First, the higher animals and the domestic animals, such as the dog, the horse and the elephant.

Secondly, the so-called wild animals, such as the lion, the tiger, and the other carnivorous and dangerous wild animals.

Thirdly, the mass of lesser animals that seem to meet no particular need nor to fill any special purpose, such as the harmless yet multitudinous lives found in our forests, our jungles and the fields of our planet. Instances of these in the West are the rabbits and other rodents. This is a wide and general specification of no scientific import at all; but it covers adequately the karmic divisions and the general conformation into

which these groupings of lives fall in this
kingdom.

Objective
agency . . . . . . Fire and Water,—fierce desire and incipient
mind. These are symbolised in the animal
power to eat and drink.

Subjective
agency . . . . . . Smell or Scent,—the instinctual discovery
of that which is needed, from the activity of
ranging forth for food and the use of the
power to scent that food, to the identifica-
tion of the smell of a beloved master and
friend.

Quality . . . . . Tamas or Inertia,—but in this case it is the
tamasic nature of mind and not that of mat-
ter, as usually understood. The chitta or
mind-stuff can be equally tamasic.

Esoteric Psychology I, pp. 251-54

Throat centre . . . Animal . . . 3rd ray . . . 3rd root-race . . .
Intellect; the goal.
- The energy of Illumination. Creating in the light.
- Four centres functioning.
- Focal point of the instinctual consciousness.
- The third kingdom in nature.

Esoteric Astrology, p. 455

THE INCOMING SEVENTH RAY
AND THE ANIMAL KINGDOM

1. The animal kingdom is to the human body what the dense physical body is to the seven principles.
2. The animal kingdom is the mother aspect, prior to the overshadowing of the Holy Ghost.
3. The animal kingdom is the field of individualisation.
4. Since Atlantean days the animal kingdom has been occupied with the development of karma.
5. Domestic animals constitute the heart centre in the life of the Entity Who ensouls the animal kingdom.
6. The animal kingdom does not react strongly to the 7th ray.
7. The human kingdom does, but the 7th ray will have three effects in relation to the two kingdoms and their interplay:
   a. It will refine the animal bodies.
   b. It will bring about a closer relation between men and animals.
   c. It will cause a great destruction of the present animal forms.

Esoteric Psychology I, p.415

CONNECTIONS BETWEEN THE KINGDOMS

The Building Entities

Quality	Entity	Centre	Personality	Kingdom	
1. Atma	Logos	Head (Brain)	Grand Heavenly Man	Seventh	Unity
2-3 Buddhi manas	Planetary Logos	Heart and Throat	Heavenly Men	Sixth and Fifth	Duality
4. Mental	Man	Solar Plexus Base of the Spine	Man	Fourth	Triplicity
5. Astral	Animal	Generative Organs		Third	Duality
6. Etheric	Vegetable	Spleen		Second	Transitional
7. Dense	Mineral	None		First	Unity

A Treatise on Cosmic Fire, p. 565

If the table [on the previous page] is carefully studied, it will be seen that the fivefold earlier enumeration concerns the most important kingdoms in nature, whilst the final two are peculiarly interesting in that the mineral kingdom can in no sense be considered a principle, but simply the densest point of concretion of the abstract, and that the vegetable kingdom has a peculiar place in the economy of the system as the transmitter of the vital pranic fluid; the vegetable kingdom is definitely a bridge between the conscious and the unconscious. Here I am using these words in their broadest and most general sense. Though it is known that the mineral kingdom has a consciousness of its own, yet *sensation* is more distinctly recognisable in the second kingdom, and the distinction between the consciousness of the mineral and that of the animal is so vast that their respective consciousnesses are basically unlike. Between these stands the vegetable kingdom, approximating more generally the animal consciousness than the mineral, and having a most esoteric relationship to the deva evolution.

A Treatise on Cosmic Fire, pp. 564

. . . The vegetable kingdom similarly provides the negative energy for the astral permanent atom of a man, and thirdly, the animal kingdom provides the negative force which when energised by the positive is seen as the mental unit. This energy which is contributed by the three lower kingdoms is formed of the very highest vibration of which that kingdom is capable, and serves as a link between man and his various sheaths, all of which are allied to one or other of the lower kingdoms.

a. The mental body . . . mental unit . . . animal kingdom.
b. The astral body . . . . astral . . . . vegetable kingdom.
               permanent
               atom
c. The physical body . . physical . . . . . mineral kingdom.
               permanent
               atom

In man these three types of energy are brought together, and synthesised, and when perfection of the personality is reached, and the vehicles aligned, we have:

a. The energy of the mental unit . . . . positive.
b. The energy of the astral
   permanent atom . . . . equilibrised.
c. The energy of the physical
   permanent atom . . . . negative.

Man is then closely linked with the three lower kingdoms by the best that they can provide, and they have literally given him his permanent atoms, and enabled him to manifest through their activity. The above three groups might be studied also from the standpoint of the three Gunas:

1. Tamas . . inertia . . . . mineral kingdom . . . . physical
                                      permanent
                                      atom.
2. Rajas . . . activity . . . vegetable kingdom . . astral
                                      permanent
                                      atom.
3. Sattva . . rhythm . . . animal kingdom . . . . mental unit.

All these must be regarded only from the point of view of the personality, the lower self, or not-self. In illustration of this idea, it might be pointed out that when the animal body of prehuman man was rhythmically adjusted, and had attained its highest or sattvic vibration, then individualisation became possible, and a true human being appeared in manifestation.

A Treatise on Cosmic Fire, pp. 1134-35

THE RAYS AND THE KINGDOMS IN NATURE

The kingdoms which we shall consider in connection with the rays may be enumerated under the following terms:

1. The Mineral Kingdom VII
2. The Vegetable Kingdom VI
3. The Animal Kingdom V
4. The Kingdom of Men IV
5. The Kingdom of Souls III
6. The Kingdom of Planetary Lives II
7. The Kingdom of Solar Lives I

These kingdoms might be regarded as differentiations of the One Life, from the angle of:

1. Phenomenal appearance, objective manifestation, or the externalisation of the solar Logos.
2. Consciousness or sensitivity to the expression of quality, through the medium of the phenomenal appearance.

Certain of the rays, as might be expected, are more responsible than certain others for the qualifying of any particular kingdom. Their effect is paramount in its determination. The effect of the other rays is subsidiary, but not absent. We must never forget that, in the close interrelation of forces in our solar system, no one of the seven possible forces is without effect. All of them function, qualify and motivate, but one or other will have a more vital effect than the rest. The following tabulation will give the major effect of the seven rays and the result of their influence upon the seven kingdoms with which we are concerned:

No.	Kingdom	Ray	Expression
1.	Mineral	VII. Ceremonial	Organisation Radio-Activity.
		I. Will or Power	The basic Reservoir of Power.
2.	Vegetable	II. Love-Wisdom	Magnetism.
		IV. Beauty or Harmony	Uniformity of Colour.
		VI. Idealistic Devotion	Upward Tendency.
3.	Animal	III. Adaptability	Instinct.
		VI. Devotion	Domesticity.

Esoteric Psychology I, pp. 215–16

The rays of attribute, though expressing themselves equally on all the planes and through the periodical vehicles and the three aspects of the personality, find their main expression through one or other of the four kingdoms in nature:

Ray IV . . Harmony, Conflict . . . . 4th kingdom . . . . Human.

The Balance.

Ray V . . . Concrete Knowledge . . 3rd kingdom . . . . Animal.

Ray VI . . Devotion . . . . 2nd kingdom . . . Vegetable.

Ray VII . Ceremonial Ritual . . . . 1st kingdom . . . . Mineral.

Esoteric Psychology I, p. 162

THE FIVE SECRETS OF THE KINGDOMS IN NATURE

There is a secret anent each of the five kingdoms in nature. These secrets concern the relation of the human evolution to the whole, and they are revealed to the initiate at the five initiations. At each initiation one of the five secrets is explained to the initiate, and they are called by the following five names, which are an attempt on my part to interpret symbolically the ancient name or sign:

1. The mineral kingdom . . . . . The secret of the brilliance of the light.
2. The vegetable kingdom . . . The secret of the sacred perfume.
3. The animal kingdom . . . . . The secret of the following scent.
4. The human kingdom . . . . . The secret of the double path or of the double breath.
5. The kingdom of souls . . . . . The secret of the golden rose of light.

The symbolic forms in which these five secrets are hidden, and so conveyed to the intelligence of the initiate, are as follows:

1. The mineral secret . . . A diamond, blue white in colour.
2. The vegetable secret . . A cube of sandalwood in the
   heart of the lotus.
3. The animal secret . . . . A bunch of cypress, over a
   funeral urn.
4. The human secret . . . . A twisted golden cord, with
   seven knots.
5. The egoic secret . . . . . A closed lotus bud with seven
   blue rays.

Ibid., pp. 238-39

THE SCIENCE OF THE RAYS AND THE FOUR KINGDOMS

The four kingdoms in nature are embodiments of four great Lives Who are found, each on one of the four minor rays. . . . The Being Who ensouls similarly the third kingdom, the animal kingdom, vibrates to the sixth ray. The Being Who is the expression and active force of the entire vegetable kingdom is to be found upon the fourth ray. Therefore we have:

Humanity . . . 4th Kingdom . . 5th Ray . . . Concrete
Knowledge.

Animal . . . . . 3rd Kingdom . . 6th Ray . . . Devotion
upwards or
forwards.

Vegetable . . . 2nd Kingdom . . 4th Ray . . . Harmony and
Beauty.

Mineral. . . . . 1st Kingdom . . 7th Ray . . . Organisation
and Ritual.

Ibid., pp. 120-21

ARCANE SCHOOL TRAINING

Training for new age discipleship is provided

by the *Arcane School*. The principles of the

Ageless Wisdom are presented through esoteric

meditation, study and service as a *way of life*.

****

www.lucistrust.org/arcaneschool